PLANETS TELL YOUR FUTURE

R.H. Bhanot

Books For All
[A Division of D.K. Publishers Distributors (P) Ltd.]
Delhi - 110 052

Sales Office:
D.K. Publishers Distributors (P) Ltd.
1, Ansari Road, Darya Ganj
New Delhi- 110 002
Phone: 3261465, 3278368
Fax: 091-011-3264368

ISBN 81-7386-149-8

Published by:
BOOKS FOR ALL
[A Division of D.K. Publishers Distributors (P) Ltd.]
Regd Office: A-6, NIMRI Community Centre
Ashok Vihar Phase IV, Near Bharat Nagar
Delhi-110052
Phone: 7143353, 7430113
Fax: 091-011-7138265

Printed at:
D.K. Fine Art Press (P) Ltd., Delhi - 110 052

PRINTED IN INDIA

PREFACE

The need for a general book on astrology which would be useful for the lay man and also for the advanced student or practitioner was brought home to me during a casual survey of the books available in the market. Many of these books published in the west were admirable efforts in their own way but were based on the movable or tropical zodiac or else were written only on the basis of the Sun sign, that is the sign occupied by the Sun. As I have also explained in this book, the Sun sign is only one of the several important influences that bear on one's nativity. The Moon sign is equally important and also the *house* occupied by the Sun or Moon. And the house positions of the other planets, the signs they occupy and their mutual relationship all play their part in forming one's character and destiny in life.The *directions* or dashas give an idea of when a particular event will manifest itself. Western scholars are able to draw some conclusions on the basis of aspects and sometimes also from the progressed horoscope.

The lay man is normally not able to follow the calculations involved in working out the aspects and the progressions. In the present work I have based my study on the Sidereal or fixed Zodiac and have also explained how one can work out the periods or *dashas* as per the systems named after the sage Parashar. There are other systems based on the 108 year cycle or on the *yoginis* but the Parashari cycle of 120 years has gained general acceptance in India on the basis of its generally correct results and the reader of this book will be able to work out the periods and sub-periods of this Dasha system for himself without any elaborate calculation.

To the sceptic all I can say is: Read the book with an open mind and apply some of the principles to the charts of friends and relatives of whose life and character you have some idea. You will find in all cases, provided their charts are correctly drawn up, that there is a close relationship between the planetary configurations in their charts and the actual events in their lives. Even if you do not believe everything the astrologer says, you cannot deny that there is a close relationship between the events of one's life and astrological prognostications regarding their timing as the great Austrian psychologist Karl Jung had also admitted.

I have no doubt the book will stand on its own merit and give the reader much useful information and a deeper understanding of human character and destiny. Such a comprehensive yet concise work on astrology has not been brought out so far and should therefore find a place in every household, to be referred to periodically and at leisure.

Dehradun **R.H. Bhanot**
June 17, 1995

The Uniqueness Of The Work

The books on the subject of astrology published in the west are usually based only on the Sun sign, though the Sun is only one of the factors in one's natal chart. Other books go into aspects based on the western system, including progressed horoscopes. These become very detailed and technical and the lay reader is unable to profit by them.

The books published in India contain references to Sanskrit publications or are written in a ponderous style thus putting off the lay reader. My work is easy to read and clearly explains the western and the Indian approach, so that readers both in the east and the west can profit by it. This will be clear from the chapter on 'Aspects and on the Signs.' The nakshatra system is explained in simple language so that the reader is able to work out the dasha for himself. Some time tested principles are explained and can be referred to by readers again and again .

All in all, the work is a guide to astrology, a handy book of reference and a work that gives one a deep insight into astrology. No reader, on completing the book, will ever be the same person again, so pervasive is its influence. It teaches us to take a wide view of the human situation and generates compassion towards humanity, producing in us Peace, and Peace and again Peace.

Such a concise yet comprehensive book on astrology has never been produced so far.

R.H. Bhanot

CONTENTS

Where Does The Circle Begin?

There are some basic astronomical facts with which every one interested in astrology has to become familiar. The Sun moves approximately one degree every day. This is an apparent motion, due to the revolution of the earth around the Sun and the line of sight from an observer on the earth to the Sun and the heavens beyond will end at a point which moves from west to east at the rate of about one degree every day. Thus the sun seems to move from Aries to Taurus in about a month and to Gemini in another month and so on till after one year it comes back to the starting point.

Now where should we begin—where do we place the First Point of Aries where the Sun's motion will be taken to start in its journey along the ecliptic? (Ecliptic is the path of the Sun in the heavens). Now the ecliptic is a circle in the heavens and so is the equator. Two circles inclined to each other will intersect at only two points. The Sun moves from the south to the north of the equator till the spring equinox on the twenty-first March when it crosses the equator. On its southward journey it again crosses the equator on the twenty-third September. It is farthest south on the twenty-second December when it slowly commences its northward journey.

Western astrologers take 21st March as the base point for marking out the Zodiac and say that on this day the Sun comes to the first degree of Aries - thus it is in the First Point of Aries. It moves one degree every day and in a month's time enters the first degree of Taurus. The first point of Aries is thus the point at which the ecliptic intersects the equator in the northward journey of the Sun. This is the point of commencement of the Zodiac and the beginning of the first of the twelve signs, which are then calculated at 30^0 per sign. All these signs fall within the great Zodiacial circle for the purposes of the astrologers. The zodiac may be taken as a belt in the heavens of about 15^0 in width, $7½^0$ north and south of the equator and all our planets, however much they wander about in the skies forever remain within this 15^0 broad path, $7½^0$ north and south of the ecliptic.

Few astrologers know that the First point of Aries is itself in motion though very slowly, at the rate of about 50 seconds of arc per year or nearly 1 degree in 6 years. Many people will be surprised to learn that the great Varahmihira who lived about fifteen centuries ago had been able to give this figure of 50" which corresponds closely to the figure given by modern astronomers. Considering that Varahmihira had no tools available to him, no telescopes or other equipment, his achievements in the realm of astrology are remarkable. He was a man of many-sided genius, comparable to Leonardo da Vinci, who too was a painter, a sculptor, an engineer, an inventor and all in all truly a superman in many respects. So was Varahmihira, of whom India can be truly proud.

Hindu astrology follows the Fixed Zodiac and not the movable or tropical zodiac. The Hindu system takes the group of stars called Aswini as the first point or degree of Aries. As the tropical system follows the movable Zodiac and as the point at which the ecliptic crosses the celestial equator moves backwards at about 50 seconds per year, there must have been a time when the tropical first point of Aries was also in the Aswini group of stars, that is, there must have been a time when the commencing point of Aries was the same in both the systems.

This date has been taken to be

213 A.D. by Fagan

285 A.D. by Lahiri

397 A.D. by Raman

345 A.D. by Khareghat and

291 A.D. by Krishnamurti.

Opinion is strongly divided, as we can see from the above dates. Nevertheless, we have to accept that there was a time, about 15 to 18 centuries ago, when the tropical or movable Zodiac coincided with the fixed Zodiac in which the First Point of Aries is in the asterism Aswini and which the Sun enters on the 13th April every year and from which all the signs are calculated.

In most newspapers the astrological columnist goes by the Movable Zodiac and takes it that the sign Aries begins from the Sun's position in the heavens on the 21st March and he gives a few readings on the basis of the Sun's position in one's birth chart. For instance, the columnist will proceed to place in Aries the location of Sun and will give some "reading" which may titillate us but which in effect is of little value because Sun is only one of the agents affecting us. Moon is another and equally important and could be in any of the twelve signs of the Zodiac on the 21st March. So also the Ascendant, which is no less important and could be in any of the twelve signs of the Zodiac on the 21st March (or on any other day) according to the time of birth. Thus, for one born at sunrise when the Sun is in Aries on the 21st March and for the next one month, one's ascendant will also be Aries. Two hours after sunrise, the ascendant will be Taurus and about four hours later it will be in Gemini and the Sun will have moved to the eleventh house and so on till the following morning when some time before sunrise the ascendant will be Pisces, the twelfth zodiacal sign.

In the Hindu System, Sun will still be in Pisces on the 21st March and one born at Sunrise on that day will be a sun Piscean (and not Sun Aries as in the Western system) and also will have Pisces as ascendant. The importance of all this can be realised when we bear in mind, for instance, that Pisces is a watery sign, it is mutable, mute, negative as against Aries which is fiery, movable, barren, violent and positive. Readings based on the two systems will thus be very different and the reader will be a bit puzzled at the many discrepancies in two sets of readings, one based on the fixed Zodiac and the other on the movable zodiac.

My advice to the reader will be to choose one system and experience will enable him gradually to understand and interpret charts in course of time. There is a large amount of astrological literature covering both systems. I follow the Hindu system for one important reason among others. This is the system of periods or *Dashas* in it which is totally absent in the movable Zodiac system.

The *dasha* system as we will learn later in this book, is another major contribution of Hindu astrology, to relate the results of astrological positions of planets in a chart to the life span of the subject and in particular to time the events, favourable or otherwise, that one can expect over the years following birth.

In this book I have followed the fixed Zodiac throughout except where otherwise stated. Thus, the signs and the location of planets in them are all based on the Fixed Zodiac. Thus, when Aries is mentioned it is taken as the part of the Zodiac extending from the point in the asterism Aswini which is the beginning of the Fixed Zodiac to the part of the zodiac ending 30^0 later when Taurus begins. Aries is also the part of the heavens in which the Sun moves from the 13th April every year onwards for the next one month. Similarly Gemini begins from the position the Sun occupies on the 15th June every year and ends after 30°. A person born, say, on the 25th June will have Sun in about 10° of Gemini and will be generally a person with Gemini qualities whereas the followers of the Moving Zodiac system will place him as a Cancer subject because they take it that Sun is in Cancer from the 21st June onwards to the 21st July.

An important argument in favour of the fixed Zodiac system is the position of the stars in the heavens which do not change appreciably over time as humanity knows it. The sign Taurus for example is visualised as the Bull because in the heavens the stars are so positioned that one feels that the two horns of the bull are out there. The sign Sagittarius is half animal and half human as if the torso of a man is aiming an arrow. Leo appears as if a lion is located out there in the sky; Pisces is like two fishes close together, curved and with their backs to each other. These signs do not change from century to century and if, as astrologers believe, some kind of cosmic radiation comes towards us from the heavens, the nature of such radiation varies from sign to sign. In other words we can take it that this radiation affects us differently if we are born under different signs—whether it is by virtue of the Sun's position, or the ascendant, or the position of the Moon or of the other planets. Thus Gemini is an airy sign, it is variable and is governed by Mercury the fast moving messenger pictured as a two faced person, talkative, humourous, inconstant. Gemini influence thus is quite different say from Cancer, which is a watery sign, quick to absorb outside influences and change according to the nature of these influences, just as water becomes coloured according to the substance that dissolves in it. Now Gemini appears to us like twins or two persons standing close to each other out there in the heavens. We can best observe the signs on a cloudless sky, after a shower has settled all the dust in the atmosphere and in particular from a hill station where the stars shine with a special brilliance. One who sees the heavens under such conditions comes under the spell of the heavens and is swayed by the emotion of Wonder which we in modern times are beginning to forget and lose as we come under the influence of mega cities, highrise buildings, dust and smog in the air, the all prevading noise and hum of traffic and also by the purely intellectual and analytical approach to life.

The heavens are a beautiful sight at night and the signs we observe in it are fixed and unchanging as far as human time goes. But if we proceed on the basis of the moving Zodiac, the signs lose their special patterns as observed by the human eye over the past four or five thousand years. As I have said above, the sign Aries under the fixed Zodiac system of the Indians no longer remains the same when we follow the tropical or moving Zodiac. The first degree of Aries becomes the 23rd degree, the preceding 22 odd degrees being of Pisces of the fixed system. Similarly for the other signs. The beautiful patterns as we have pictured them for thousands of years become disturbed, as if we had cut them and sliced off parts of every one of them and joined a part to another sign. Thus Leo, corresponding to the majestic lion will have his head cut off and joined to Cancer, the crab. Will the sign still stand for the Lion and partake of its notable and kingly nature or become partly a crab moving in an ungainly fashion partly forward and partly sideways, very emotional, quick to absorb outside influences?

The Moving Zodiac breaks up the twelve signs in a manner which some how disturbs the *gestalt*, the pattern as we see it in the skies. The pattern is as under.

Aries; the first sign is the Ram, aggressive and poised always to attack with its short curving horns. It is symbolised by its horns thus ♈

Taurus, the placid Bull symbolised by ♉

Gemini, the inconstant Twins symbolised by ♊

Cancer, the Crab symbolised by ♋

Leo the kingly Lion, symbolised by ♌

Virgo, the Virgin, symbolised by ♍

Libra, the balanced and justice-loving scales, symbolised by ♎

Scorpio, the sarcastic scorpion who can sting by his words and who is determined and tenacious and is symbolised by the symbol ♏

Sagittarius, the optimistic and honorable Archer, whose symbol is ♐

Capricorn the cautious, persevering and shrewd crocodile symbolised by the symbol ♑

Aquarius or the Waterpot, humane and faithful, symbolised by ♒

Pisces or the Fishes, quiet and tactful and symbolised appropriately by ♓

A more detailed study of the twelve signs will be undertaken in the later chapters of this book when we will also discuss the twelve houses into which an astrological chart is divided. We will close this chapter with some more remarks on the Fixed and Movable Zodiacs.

The major part of the English speaking world seems to follow the Moving or Tropical Zodiac in which the First Point of Aries is the point occupied by the Sun on the 21st March every year when it comes to the point of intersection of the ecliptic and the celestial equator in its northward journey. In India for thousands of years the Fixed Zodiac has been followed. In the Tropical system the First point of Aries is easy to fix as it can be scientifically worked out by rules of astronomy. The fixed system, on the contrary, offers some problems in arriving at the first point of Aries. Our ancients, not having any of the tools of astronomical sciences went by their visual observations and started the circle of the Zodiac from the group of stars known as Aswini, so named because it appears like the head of a horse. Now this group of stars extends over a few degrees but the astrologer wants greater accuracy to within minutes and seconds of arc. The ancients therefore proceeded from the bright star Spica, visible to the naked eye, at the end of the sign Virgo and worked backwards 180° to come to the first degree of Aries where they located the beginning of Aries and indeed of the fixed Zodiac.

Now all Western tables such as the Almanacs published in US and in Europe give the position of planets according to the Tropical Zodiac. To apply them to the Indian sysyem we have to deduct the *Ayanamsa* which for the year 1995 may be taken as 23° and 41'. This is to be deducted in each and every case—for the position of planets as also for the house positions given in various Tables of Houses. I may add that there is some difference of opinion in this matter, for Lahiri gives 23° and 46' as the difference to be deducted from the Tropical system figures.

The Ayanamsa varies from year to year as I have said above, at the rate of 5' every six years. For the year 1900 it was 22° 22', for 1906 it was 22° 27', for 1950 it was 23° 4'. For the year 2000 it will be 23° 46'. In casting a horoscope from Sayana or moving

Zodiac tables and ephemeris we must deduct the Ayanamsa to arrive at the fixed system charts based on the Nirayana (or without *ayana*) system also known as the sidereal system followed in this book.

To sum up the position, the Tropical or Moving Zodiac system is not satisfactory to the Indian astrologer as it seems to violate the nature of the twelve signs as they appear to the naked eye, the Ram, the Bull, the Twins, the Crab and so on, ending with Pisces, the Fishes, and secondly it is of no use when it comes to a study of the 27 asterisms or Nakshatras which govern the various dashas or periods of planets, commencing from the period of the nakshatra in which the Moon was located at birth.

In the following chapters we will study these Nakshatras as well as the twelve signs and the twelve houses of the birth chart, beginning with the signs which are the 30^0 units of the Zodiac and the importance of which had been realised by the Chaldeans, Assyrians, Babylonians, Egyptians and Greeks as is also realised by astrologers of the modern times.

Kala Purusha Or Cosmic Man

Among the major contributions of India to astrology is the concept of *Kala Purusha* or Cosmic man. The concept brings together the astrological signs and the various parts of the human body and helps us to understand the relationship of the signs and the human body. Thus, the first sign Aries with which the Zodiac starts both in the Hindu or Indian astrology and western astrology, corresponds to the head and any adverse planets in Aries can affect the head. Taurus, the second sign of the Zodiac is the throat of *Kala Purusha.* The arms and shoulders are Gemini. Cancer is the chest and lungs and adverse influences in Cancer can result in some malady of the respiratory system. Leo is the heart of *Kala Purusha* and Virgo the Stomach, intestine and the digestive system in general. Virgo is also the sixth sign counted from Aries and the sixth house, as all astrologers know, is related to health and disease.

One will realise that Virgo is very important in understanding the causation and nature of disease where it is affected by malefic planets or planetary influences. For example, Virgo will correspond to the sixth house for those born when Aries was rising and if in the chart of such persons, Mars, Saturn, Rahu and Ketu or one or two of them are located in Virgo, such a person may suffer from troubles related to the bowels or the digestive system. Mars and Ketu may even result in surgery such as in Hernia. In any case such an influence will be indicative of dysentery, diarrhoea, gas, pain in the region of the stomach, ulcer in the stomach, wound or injury etc. Now one can ask why in the digestive system; why not in the arms or in the chest? *Kala Purusha* explains why, for the sixth house and Virgo are the digestive system, intestines, bowels of *Kala Purusha* and if this house and sign are afflicted, some sort of trouble of this part or system follows. This is a logical effect of the concept and no intuition or far fetched theory is required to explain it.

We will find again and again that many logial conclusions follow from some basic postulates of astrology and it is therefore entirely erroneous on the part of those whose aquaintance with astrology is non-existent to affirm that astrology is nothing but a bundle of superstitions. Unfortunately many otherwise brilliant scientists hold this view. I can only plead with them to come to the subject with an open mind. If they do so, they will not fail to be impressed by the subject as with the concept of *Kala Purusha.*

The seventh sign Libra corresponds to the seventh house where the kidneys, the genitals and the small of the back are located. This is an extremely important region because sex is, after hunger, the most important driving force in us—in some respects it is even more important than hunger, particularly in the modern age where sex is dominating practically all our important cultural values. If the seventh house is afflicted, say, by Ketu and Saturn, one's reproductive system, marriage and married life are bound to be affected. Here too, I would like to draw the attention of those who pooh-pooh Indian astrology and refer to it in contemptuous terms to the perfectly logical conclusions that the astrologer draws from the basic principles in the same manner as a physical scientist does in his field of study. There is nothing superstitious here. If the seventh house is afflicted, without any benefic aspect to it or its lord, the native will, *without fail* suffer the adverse results I have mentioned above. I have come across many instances of Ketu, Saturn, Rahu and Mars afflicting the seventh house and without exception they had some problems or troubles with their marriage, partner, sexual system, fertility or virility or sexually transmitted diseases. There is no superstition here nor any element of chance. Evil planetary influences in the seventh house will, without exception, and in the same manner as in physical sciences cause or at least be related to adverse functioning of the seventh house matters. Let a 'pure' scientist study this matter with an unbiased mind and he will not be able to deny that a connection exists whether causal or otherwise, between malefic influences in the seventh house and troubles of the reproductive system.

Also there can be adverse results in other fields of activity. Thus, I have come across many instances of Saturn in the seventh in charts of otherwise normal women who could not get married until quite late in life. Our girls are usually married off at the age of 20 to 25 years or even earlier, but if Saturn is in the seventh house of women, their marriage is delayed. I have come across such cases even abroad in the U.S.A. too. In some cases the marriage does not come about at all. In others there is coldness between the partners—note that Saturn is a planet of coldness, delays, despondency among other things.

Even Sun, the kingly planet in the seventh can cause adverse results though not of the types associated with the major malefics. Sun in the Seventh can result in some interruption of an otherwise normal married life. This is the case of a girl married to an Army Colonel, when Sun *dasha* or period started, the husband was posted to a non-family station in Ladakh and she took a job as Principal of a girls public school started by a Maharani. Here the adverse influence or effect was not related to health or finances—all the same the smooth flow of happy married life was interrupted, although for a short period, until the Colonel had completed his stay in Ladakh and came back to a "family" station.

I have given above some instances of adverse influence over the seventh house. There can however, also be as many cases of benefic planets, aspecting or affecting the seventh house. Thus, if the great benefic Jupiter is located in the seventh in a favourable sign and if it is also associated with a benefic Moon, such a native will have a beautiful and noble wife who will be a source of joy to all who came in contact with her. Venus similarly placed in the seventh will also give him a beautiful, amorous and wealthy wife. Mercury in the seventh is a good indication for business matters, for good humour and matters governed by Mercury.

The eighth house and Scorpio are the excretory parts of *Kala Purusha* and Mars and Ketu may be indicative of such troubles as Piles.

The ninth house is the thighs of *Kala Purusha*. A planet like Jupiter in the ninth or in Sagittarius which is the ninth sign may indicate long and well-formed thighs as of footballers. I myself have such a placement of Jupiter and I was in my time a footballer and I will not hesitate to say that many women admired my thighs even in massage bath parlours—these women in the course of their professional duties had occasion to see hundreds of men and an unsolicited testimonial from them over my thighs certainly meant something.

Jupiter in Sagittarius, the 9th sign of the Zodiac gives very well formed and long thighs. In interpreting the results of planetary configurations one should remember that the theory or hypothesis of *Kala Purusha* has particular reference to the signs—thus Aries is the first sign and stands for the head of *Kala Purusha*.

For one born with the ascendant in Cancer, the fourth sign, it would not be proper to say that the first house (in this case Cancer) stands for the head. Cancer is the fourth sign representing the breast region of *Kala Purusha.* Though Cancer here is in a way also representative of the head, it is primarily the breast or chest region and evil planets here (in Cancer) predominantly affect the breast or chest. Thus, in a Cancer ascendant subject related to me, with Mars and Rahu in Cancer the nipples were rudimentary and she had great difficulty in feeding her child. Saturn's aspect to Cancer made matter worse. Eventhough the doctor in-charge advised massage and gentle pull applied several times a day to the nipples, the problem continued even when the second child was born. This shows the importance of natal influences, which cannot always be put aside by human efforts and ultimately we all have to learn to live with them.

The tenth sign is Capricorn which forms the knees of *Kala Purusha.* Evil influences here could result in problems related to the knees such as rheumatism or arthritis. Here one should also remember that Capricorn is ruled by Saturn which stands for old age, bones and all chronic diseases. Saturn also stands for Aquarius, the eleventh sign governing the legs between the knees and ankles. Some western astrologers give to Uranus the rulership over Aquarius. Uranus was unknown to Indians, when astrological principles were first laid down. Indeed Uranus was unknown even in the Western world until quite late in the day. When Ptolemy first compiled the then known principles of astrology about two thousand years ago and brought together in a book all the knowledge of the subject from Assyrian and Babylonian times onwards, Uranus and other trans-Saturn planets were unknown as no telescopes were available then to astrologers. As we will learn later in this book, inspite of this handicap, the ancients were able to put together some remarkable facts (based on intuition shall we say?). For instance the Greeks must have formed some idea of the twin nature of Mercury which always shows the same face to the Sun, just as Moon does to the Earth. Thus, Mercury is half shining and half totally dark. How the ancient Greeks learnt of this is a mystery.

Finally *Kala Purusha* stands on Pisces which are the feet. Pisces as we know is the twelfth sign.

In talking of the order of the signs, we come to the complex question of where the signs begin, which is the starting point of the Zodiac or 0^0 of the Ecliptic or the great circle of the heavens within which all planets move, forward or backward, north or south of the celestial equator. Here I would only like to mention once again that the theory of *Kala Purusha* is a unique and distinctive contribution of Hindus to the branch of knowledge known as astrology, a contribution of which India can be proud.

One other contribution made by Indian Scholars of ancient times might be mentioned here, though unconnected with the concept of *Kala Purusha.* This is the view clearly expressed by Aryabhatt who was born in 476 A.D. and who has stated in his work "Aryabhatiya" that the Sun and the stars are fixed and that "day and night are caused by the rotation of the earth." This was about a thousand years *before* the age of Galileo and Copernicus to whom credit has been given in the West for discovering that the heavens do not go round the earth which stays put.

Nakshatras Or Asterisms

As I have explained earlier, the 15^0 wide belt in which the ecliptic or the Sun's path in the heavens as well as the paths of all the planets and also of Rahu and Ketu (Dragon's Head and Tail) are located, is divided into 12 signs each of 30^0, beginning with Aries. The signs are ruled by different Planets as under:

Aries	ruled by	Mars	symbol	♂
Taurus	ruled by	Venus	symbol	♀
Gemini	ruled by	Mercury	symbol	☿
Cancer	ruled by	Moon	symbol	☽
Leo	ruled by	Sun	symbol	☉
Virgo	ruled by	Mercury	symbol	☿
Libra	ruled by	Venus	symbol	♀
Scorpio	ruled by	Mars	symbol	♂
Sagittarius	ruled by	Jupiter	symbol	♃
Capricorn	ruled by	Saturn	symbol	♄
Aquarius	ruled by	Saturn	symbol	♄
Pisces	ruled by	Jupiter	symbol	♃

Many astrologers, particularly in Europe and America, give to Uranus rulership over Aquarius. Neptune and Pluto have not been given any rulership.

From the above we can see that the Sun and Moon each rule over one sign, the other planets Mercury, Venus, Mars, Saturn and Jupiter are allotted two signs each.

If Sun and Moon are placed at the centre, to either side we will see Mercury, Venus and Mars as rulers followed by Jupiter ruling over Sagittarius and Saturn over the next two signs and then Jupiter again for the last sign. If we place the signs in a circle beginning with Sun and Moon, we will see on either side Mercury, Venus, Mars, Jupiter and Saturn.

If visualised in a straight line with the Moon and Sun at the centre, we find to the right the planet Mercury (nearest to the Sun) ruling Virgo which is next to Leo ruled by Sun. Venus whose orbit is next to that of Mercury rules the sign Libra next to Virgo, Mars comes next after Venus and it rules the next sign Scorpio, followed by Jupiter ruling Sagittarius and then Saturn ruling Capricorn, Saturn being the most distant planet visible to the naked eye. To the left next to Moon is again Mercury ruling Gemini, the sign before Cancer,. then comes Venus again ruling Taurus followed by Mars ruling Aries, Jupiter ruling Pisces and Saturn ruling Aquarius. Clearly there is order in the rulership assigned to the planets and signs, according to the distance of the planets from the Sun.

Every sign is divided into Nakshatras, each of 13^0 20'. *Nakshatras* are ruled by different planets in the same way as Signs or Rashis are ruled. Thus, Aries is ruled by Mars but when it is divided into Nakshatras, the first Nakshatra is Aswini ruled not by Mars the sign lord but by Ketu. The next Nakshatra also of 13^0 20' is called *Bharani* ruled by Venus. The remaining part of Aries of 3^0 20' is ruled by Sun as it is a part of Krittika Nakshatra over which Sun has rulership

As there are 27 Nakshatras and only nine planets, three Nakshatras are given or allocated to every planet as under :

Aswini extending from 0^0 to 13^0 20' Aries, is ruled by Ketu.

Bharani ruled by Venus extends from the end of Aswini to 26^0 40'.

Krittika, the third Nakshatra ends at 40^0 and is ruled by Sun.

Rohini is ruled by Moon and extends to 53^0 20'.

Mrigashira ruled by Mars ends at 66^0 40'.

Ardra comes next and is ruled by Rahu or Dragons Head and extends to 80^0.

Punarvasu is ruled by Jupiter and ends at 93^0 20'.

Puṣhyami extends to 106^0 40' and is ruled by Saturn.

Aslesha is ruled by Mercury and extends to another 13^0 20' ending at 120^0.

Thus, we see that four signs—Aries, Taurus, Gemini and Cancer are fully accounted for by the first nine asterisms or nakshatras, each of 13^0 20'. At the end of these nine nakshatras we begin again with Ketu, followed by Venus, Sun, Moon, Mars, Rahu, Jupiter, Saturn and Mercury in that order and the next four signs—Leo, Virgo, Libra and Scorpio are thus accounted for. The names of these nine Nakshatras are Magha, Purvaphalguni, Uttarphalguni, Hasta, Chitra, Swati, Vishaka, Anuradha and Jyestha. The signs Sagittarius, Capricorn, Aquarius and Pisces contain the next nine Nakshatras, the first of them being Moola ruled by Ketu, the next Purvashada ruled by Venus, then Uttarashada ruled by Sun and Sravana, Dhanishta, Satabhisha, Purvabhadrapad, Uttarbhadrapad and finally Revati ruled in cyclic order by Moon (Sravana), Mars, Rahu, Jupiter, Saturn and Mercury (Revati).

We see that the 27 Nakshatras completley cover all the twelve signs of the Zodiac, every sign covering 2¼ Nakshatra. The importance of these Nakshatras lies in their rulership and the position of the Moon in any Nakshatra gives us the Dasha which is operative at birth. Thus, if one is born in Hasta we will say that the Dasha of Moon was operating at birth time. Moon has rulership over Hasta, as well as over Sravana and Rohini, three Nakshatras being allotted to every planet. The Dasha or period of Moon is of 10 years and if one is born at the beginning of Hasta (or Sravana or Rohini) Moon Dasha will be running for 10 years. If one is born at a time when the Moon was at the middle of Hasta or the other two Nakshatras ruled by it, Moon period for five years will run.

A simple method to calculate dashas is to take the full extent of a nakshatra of 13½ degrees, i.e., of 800 minutes of arc and then work out the balance of the operating nakshatra by a simple calculation. Thus, if Moon is at 1^0 and 5' of a nakshatra (or 35') then the dasha that has already passed will be 35/800 of the total. If it is Moon which was operating, the dasha that has passed is 35/800 x 10, Moon dasha being of 10 years. If it was Ardra Nakshatra in which Moon was located at birth, the period that has passed will be 35/800 x 18, Ardra being ruled by Rahu whose period or Dasha is of 18 years. Having worked out the period that has passed, deduct it from the total period of the planet ruling the Nakshatra. This will give you the balance of the Dasha that will be operating at birth. The periods of the planets are as under:

Ketu	7	years
Venus	20	years
Sun	6	years
Moon	10	years
Mars	7	years
Rahu	18	years
Jupiter	16	years
Saturn	19	years
Mercury	17	years

I may add these periods or the dashas are said to have been first worked out by the sage Parashara and are named after him. There are certain other dashas also but it is the Parashari dasha that is followed these days as experience has shown that it is more accurate than others.

In every case, as I have said above, we have to take the position of Moon in degrees and minutes in any of the 27 nakshatras where it is located at birth to arrive at the dasha operating at birth. How many years and months have passed of this dasha can be worked out as shown above. We will then arrive at the balance of the period still to operate. At the end of this first operative dasha, the next period will be of the planet governing the next nakshatra, and will run for the number of years shown above against the nine planets. Thus if you are born in Sun dasha, the next will be Moon (10 years) followed by Mars (7 years), Rahu (18 years) and so on for the entire expected life span of the native.

For the convenience of the reader the Dashas and Antardashas (period and sub-periods), of all the planets beginning with Ketu are given below (in all cases the cyclic order Ketu-Venus-Sun-Moon-Mars-Rahu-Jupiter-Saturn and Mercury) has to be followed :

Moon in Ashwini (0^0 to 13^0-20') or Magha (120^0 to 133^0 - 20') or Moola (240^0 to 253^0 - 20'). Total period 7 years.

Sub- periods:-

Ketu-Ketu	4 months 27 days
Ketu-Venus	1 year 2 months
Ketu-Sun	4 months 6 days
Ketu-Moon	7 months
Ketu-Mars	4 months 27 days
Ketu-Rahu	1 year 18 days
Ketu-Jupiter	11 months 6 days
Ketu-Saturn	1 year 1 month 9 days
Ketu-Mercury	11 months 27 days

Moon in Bharani (13^0 - 20' to 26^0 - 40') or Poorvaphalguni (133^0 - 20' to 146^0 - 40') or Poorvashada (253^0 - 20' to 266^0 - 40'), all ruled by Venus whose total period is 20 years—the longest of all.

Sub - periods:-

Venus - Venus	3 years 4 months
Venus - Sun	1 year
Venus - Moon	1 year 8 months
Venus - Mars	1 year 2 months
Venus - Rahu	3 years exact
Venus - Jupiter	2 years 8 months
Venus - Saturn	3 years 2 months
Venus - Mercury	2 years 10 months
Venus - Ketu	1 year 2 months

Next in order is Sun whose total period is 6 years. The Nakshatras allotted to Sun are Krittika (26^0 40' to 40^0), Uttarphalguni (146^0 40' to 160^0) and Uttarashada (266^0 40' to 280^0). The Dasha of Sun will be operative if Moon is in any of these three Nakshatras at birth. The sub-periods of Sun are:

Sun - Sun	3 months 18 days
Sun - Moon	6 months
Sun - Mars	4 months 6 days
Sun - Rahu	10 months 24 days
Sun - Jupiter	9 months 18 days
Sun - Saturn	11 months 12 days
Sun - Mercury	10 months 6 days
Sun - Ketu	4 months 6 days
Sun - Venus	1 year exact

Moon governs Rohini (40^0 to 53^0 20'), Hasta (160^0 to 173^0 20') and Sravana (280^0 to 293^0 20'). If Moon be in any of these Nakshatras, the sub-periods of Moon dasha can be worked out as under:-

Moon - Moon	10 months
Moon - Mars	7 months
Moon - Rahu	1 year 6 months
Moon - Jupiter	1 year 4 months
Moon - Saturn	1 year 7 months
Moon - Mercury	1 year 5 months
Moon - Ketu	7 months
Moon - Venus	1 year 8 months
Moon - Sun	6 months

Mars Nakshatras are Mrigashira (53^0 20' to 66^0 40'), Chitra (173^0 20' to 186^0 40') and Dhanishta (293^0 20' to 306^0 40'), the sub-periods of Mars are as under :-

Mars - Mars	4	months 27 days
Mars - Rahu	1	year 18 days
Mars - Jupiter	11	months 6 days
Mars - Saturn	1	year 1 month 9 days
Mars - Mercury	11	months 27 days
Mars - Ketu	4	months 27 days
Mars - Venus	1	year 2 months
Mars - Sun	4	months 6 days
Mars - Moon	7	months

The Nakshatras of Rahu are Ardra (66^0 40' to 80^0), Swati (186^0 40' to 200^0) and Satabhisha (306^0 40' to 320^0) and the sub-periods of Rahu are as under:-

Rahu - Rahu	2	years 8 months 12 days
Rahu - Jupiter	2	years 4 months 24 days
Rahu - Saturn	2	years 10 months 6 days
Rahu - Mercury	2	years 6 months 18 days
Rahu - Ketu	1	years 0 months 18 days
Rahu - Venus	3	years exact
Rahu - Sun	0	year 10 months 24 days
Rahu - Moon	1	year 6 months
Rahu - Mars	1	year 0 months 18 days

If at birth Moon be in any of the three Nakshatras of Jupiter i.e., Punarvasu (80^0 to 93^0 20'), Vishaka (200^0 to 213^0 20') or Purvabhadrapada (320^0 to 333^0 20') then Jupiter dasha will be operative and its sub-periods are:-

Jupiter - Jupiter	2 years 1 month 18 days
Jupiter - Saturn	2 years 6 months 12 days
Jupiter - Mercury	2 years 3 months 6 days
Jupiter - Ketu	0 year 11 months 6 days
Jupiter - Venus	2 years 8 months
Jupiter - Sun	0 year 9 months 18 days
Jupiter - Moon	1 year 4 months 0 days
Jupiter - Mars	0 years 11 months 6 days
Jupiter - Rahu	2 years 4 months 24 days

The Dasha of Saturn operates if Moon at birth is in any of the three nakshatras ruled by Saturn which are Pushyami (93^0 20' to 106^0 40'), Anuradha (213^0 20' to 226^0 40') and Uttarbhadrapada (333^0 20' to 346^0 40') and the sub-periods of Saturn are as under:-

Saturn - Saturn	3 years 0 months 3 days
Saturn - Mercury	2 years 8 months 9 days
Saturn - Ketu	1 year 1 month 9 days
Saturn - Venus	3 years 2 months 0 days
Saturn - Sun	0 year 11 months 12 days
Saturn - Moon	1 year 7 months 0 days
Saturn - Mars	1 year 1 month 9 days
Saturn - Rahu	2 years 10 months 6 days
Saturn - Jupiter	2 years 6 months 12 days

Lastly it is Mercury which rules three Nakshatras—Aslesha (106^0 40' to 120^0), Jyestha (226^0 20' to 240^0) and Revati (346^0 40' to the end of the circle of 360^0). Its sub-periods are as under:-

Mercury - Mercury	2 years	4 months	27 days
Mercury - Ketu	0 years	11 months	27 days
Mercury - Venus	2 years	10 months	0 days
Mercury - Sun	0 years	10 months	6 days
Mercury - Moon	1 year	5 months	0 days
Mercury - Mars	0 years	11 months	27 days
Mercury - Rahu	2 years	6 months	18 days
Mercury - Jupiter	2 years	3 months	6 days
Mercury - Saturn	2 years	8 months	9 days

If the above Tables are not readily available to the astrologer, he can quickly calculate the sub-periods by multiplying the main period of the dasha lord and dasha of the lord of the sub-period, thus

Dasha lord Venus, required the length of the sub-period of say Mars.

The two figures are 20 (20 years of Venus) and 7 (Mars dasha is of seven years).

$$20 \times 7 = 140$$

Take the first two digits which give the sub-periods in months. Thus, 14 months is 1 year and two months or take Mercury and Ketu when its calculation will be as under:-

17 (Mercury dasha is of 17 years)

× 7 (Ketu main period is 7 years)

119

This gives us 11 months and the last digit is then to be multiplied by 3 to give the number of days and the final figure comes to 11 months and 27 days as the sub-period of Ketu in the main period of Mercury. This method comes in handy when you are visiting some one or when no book or table is available for reference.

It should also be noted that in all cases only the balance of the dasha remaining is to be taken, not the entire period of the dasha except where Moon is at the beginning of the Nakshatra.

Nakshatras are also associated with sounds though it is more usual to associate signs with them. Thus, the sign Virgo is associated with the sound P and many people with Virgo ascendant or Moon in Virgo have names beginning with P such as Parker, Parvati, Pratima, Peter and so on. Libra is associated with R and typical Libra individuals will have names like Richard, Robert, Rodney, Ram, Ranjan, Rajeev, Rajni etc. I do not say that this is universal and invariable but certainly it is much more common than would be the case if we were to go entirely by chance. This is something which sceptics should ponder over—why the sound R should be associated with Libra and P with Virgo.

Before we study further such interesting matters of human characteristics and signs or planets, it is necessary to be clear about certain astronomical terms and concepts which are significant in astrology too. As Evans has put it beautifully, "Astrology is an art based on Science" and we can build on the art only if the scientific basis is clear to us. In the next chapter on terminology we will study this basis in a little more detail.

TERMINOLOGY—SOME REMARKS

Among the many astronomical terms used in astrology, the first we study is Time. Astronomy proceeds on the basis of Sidereal Time, which is also used in modern astrology when casting the horoscope. Now this Sidereal time is related to the First Point of Aries. The ephemeris gives the Sidereal Time for every day of the year covered by that particular ephemeris and as the heavens go round once every twenty-four hours, Sidereal Time increases by 4 minutes every day or two hours every 30 days. Sidereal Time is given for Greenwich noon in the ephemeris published in U.K. To convert it into the time in your place of birth we have to undertake the following calculations:

First find out whether the place is east or west of Greenwich. In India, for instance, the time interval is 5½ hours between GMT and Indian Standard Time and since India is east of Greenwich, it is 5:30 p.m. here when it is noon at Greenwich. As Sidereal Time increases by 4 minutes per day or 10 seconds per hour (10 × 24 = 240 seconds or 4 minutes), we add 5½ × 10 seconds, that is 55 seconds. Further, this time interval corresponds to 360 degree of longitude, and the longitude of the place of birth is multiplied by 240/360 or 2/3. In the case of India where the Indian Standard Time is based on longitude 82 degree-30 minutes, we will multiply 82½ by 2/3 to arrive at the number of seconds to be deducted from the Sidereal Time as given in the ephemeris. Thus, the Sidereal Time for your place of birth is determined.

Further, we have to find the Local Mean Time as the Standard Time may not apply to you, unless you are born exactly at the longitude for which the Standard Time in your country is fixed. In India, for instance, you may be born at Calcutta which is at $88^0 24'$, that is about 6^0 further east and where the local mean time will therefore be 24 minutes more. Or you may be born near Bombay at Longitude 73^0 where the time interval will be about 9½ degrees into 4 minutes 0r 38 minutes less and to be deducted from the Indian Standard Time. In Philadelphia in U.S.A. the time interval is about 5 hrs less, to be deducted from G.M.T. as it is far to the west and the Sun takes about five hours to come overhead from the time it was overhead in Greenwich. It is in all cases the Local Time that you have to take to fix the position of the ascendant or the degree and the sign that was rising at the eastern horizon at the moment of birth. This ascending degree in the eastern horizon is of fundamental importance as it is the determining factor in casting the horoscopic Houses, the ascendant and the other eleven houses.

We now come to another basic problem of this time measurement that exists in India where the day is calculated from sunrise to sunrise. Traditional pundits in India who are normally relied upon by thousands of people take the moment of sunrise and give the birth time in *Ghatis*, each *ghati* being of 24 minutes duration (there being 60 *ghatis* in all in a day). A *ghati* is further divided into *vighatis*. They give the day in terms of the interval since sunrise. Thus if one is born after midnight but before the next sunrise, one will be said to be born on the previous day. If today happens to be Wednesday and one is born at 3 a.m. on the night of Wednesday and Thursaday, the Indian pundits will say that one is born on Wednesday though in fact Thursday had started at midnight.

In reading a chart drawn up by these Indian pundits, one must therefore verify the date given and make the necesary correction.

In reading such horoscopes one will come across more than one way of preparing a chart and the astrologer should know how they are prepared.

In the west a chart is prepared in a circular form thus:-

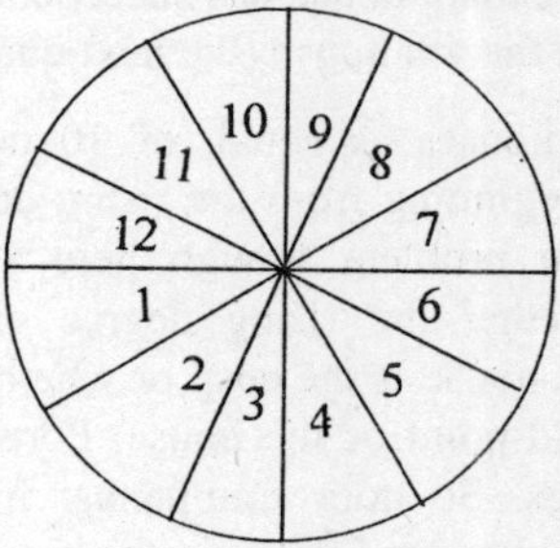

A line is drawn across the circle cutting it into two equal parts. Then a vertical line is drawn across the circle dividing the circle into four quadrants. To the left is the line showing the Ascendant sign. To the right 180^0 away is the descending sign. At the top is the zenith and the nadir is placed at the bottom. The quadrants are divided each into three parts. The line at the east is identified by the sign and the rising degree of the sign. Inside the circle close to the centre, twelve houses are marked and the rising degree of each house is given just outside the circle.

In studying these or similar charts both in India and abroad, one has to bear in mind that there are several ways in which houses are calculated. There is no difficulty in saying what the ascendant is because there can be no two opinions about the degree and sign rising at the eastern horizon at the moment of birth. 180 degrees away is the degree and sign setting on the Western horizon. Overhead is the zenith or the 10th house and at the nadir corresponding to midnight is the fourth house. The four houses 1st, 4th, 7th and 10th are easily fixed but when it is a question of the succedent and cadent houses, there are several opinions among professional astrologers (Succedent houses come just after quadrant or kendra houses, and then comes the cadent house which is just before the next quadrant. Thus, after the Ascendant house is a succedent house followed by a cadent, before the 4th house (the next quadrant).

If we take all houses as equal, of 30 degree extension, along the zodiac beginning from the rising degree of the first house, there is no problem though here again opinion is divided as to whether the rising degree or degree at the beginning of every house is the cusp or whether the cusp is to be taken as the mid-point of the house. Porphyry takes mid-points as the cusps. So does Campanus. In the system of Placidus, cusps are supposed to begin the house. In the natural graduation system too, cusps are the centres of houses. In India houses begin at cusps though this concept of cusp is not indigenous to India.

We need not get involved with the arguments of one or the other system but we may accept the view of Evans that though a house can commence at any degree of a sign and end 30 degrees beyond it, a planet in the last few degrees (say 5 degrees) of a sign affects the next sign more than it does the sign in which it infact is located. Similarly, if for instance the ascendant or the cusp of any other house is located in the last four or five degrees of the sign, it will take on the characteristics more of the next sign. Thus, for one born when the 26th degree of Virgo was rising in the Ascendant the next sign Libra will indicate his or her characteristics more than will Virgo and he or she will have more Libra characteristics than of Virgo. Similarly, for any other house and sign. This is a subject in which greater mastery can be obtained only by experience. My own experience of over 30 years impels me to accept the view of Evans in the matter.

South Latitude

South Africa, Australia, Singapore, Zimbabwe and many other English speaking countries in the southern hemisphere will be interested in casting horoscopes using tables published in the North. For them the following simple steps have to be taken:

Calculate the Sidereal Time as usual.
Add or Subtract 12 hours.

Calculate the Cusps as per the Northern Tables but change the sign into its opposite. If the northern Ascendant is Gemini we will for Southern latitudes take it as Sagittarius and so on for the Cusps of all the other houses, since we have added 12 hours to the Sidereal Time.

For the planetary positions convert this time to GMT and then find the positions of planets.

Other systems of drawing a chart may also be briefly referred to here. The system followed by the western astrologers has already been mentioned. In South India where nothing important is decided without reference to astrology, charts are prepared as under:-

Pisces	Aries	Taurus	Gemini
Aquarius			Cancer
Capricorn			Leo
Sagittarius	Scorpio	Libra	Virgo

The signs will always be as in the above maps and the astrologer will place the Ascendant in the sign in which it falls. So also the Planets and he may also give the degree and minutes of each of them.

Against this, people in North India follow the variable map or chart as below:

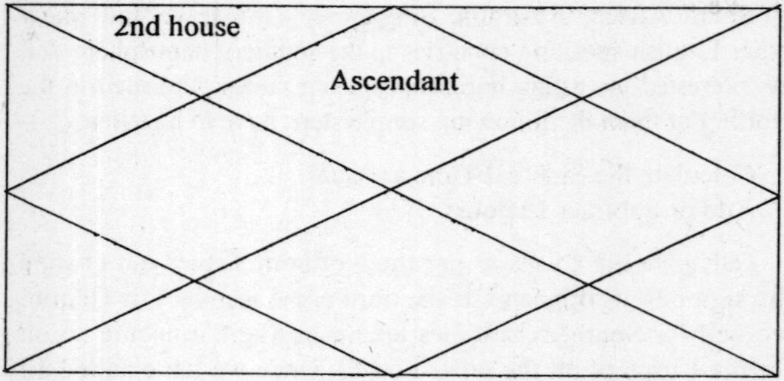

Here the houses are fixed as shown and the signs will vary. Thus, the sign in the Ascendant will be marked according to its number. For Capricorn Ascendant, for instance, the figure 10 will be entered in the first house at the top of the map, 11 in the next, to the left and so on, ending with the figure 9 standing for Sagittarius to the right of the first house or Ascendant. If Gemini is rising, the numeral 3 will be entered in the first house, 4 in the second and so on ending with 2 or Taurus in the house immediately to the right of the Ascendant.

We see from the above that while the sign position is fixed in the map drawn up by astrologers in South India, those in the North will only enter numerals standing for signs, 1 for Aries onwards to 12 for Pisces according to which sign was rising, the corresponding numeral for that sign being entered in the first house, at the top. These are only ways of drawing up the maps of the astrological chart and in no way affect the content of the chart—that is the planetary positions, signs, the ascendant and so on.

In the next section we will briefly discuss Aspects, how they are formed and what they signify. As we will see, here too there are some important differences between the Indian and Western Systems.

The Aspects

Although there is some difference in the interpretation of aspects between the Indian and the western versions, broadly both agree that the most important are the first four of the following list of aspects :

Conjunction: The symbol of which is ☌ and as the name makes it clear, it is formed when two planest are 0^0 apart.

Opposition: When the angular distance of the planets is 180 degrees and the symbol of which is ☍ .

Square: Represented by the Symbol □ and formed when angular distance is 90^0.

Trine: Shown by a triangle △ and formed when the planets are 120^0 apart.

A fifth aspect shown by the symbol ∗ is also given importance by western astrologers and is called *Sextile,* formed when the angular distance is 60^0.

The other aspects are:

Semi - Sextile	:	symbol ⊻	formed at 30^0
Semi - Square	:	symbol ∠	formed at 45^0
Sesqui-Square or Sesquiquadrate	:	symbol ⚼	formed at 135^0
Inconjunct or Quincunx	:	symbol ⚻	formed at 150^0

Quintile	:	symbol Q	formed at 72°
Semi-Quintile	:	symbol ⊥	formed at 36°
Biquintile	:	symbol ⊤	formed at 144°

Some other aspects also taken into account by astrologers are:-

Vigintile,	18° apart
Quindecile,	24° apart
Tredecile,	108° apart

Parallel, symbol P, formed when two planets are the same distance away from the celestial equator, even though they are far apart when counted from the First Point of Aries.

Western astrologers believe that planets have an *orb* of certain radius. Thus, Sun has an orb of 12° when it is applying or approaching a planet. In other words the aspect begins to be formed when the Sun is still 12° away from the point at which the aspect is fully formed. It continues to form the aspect upto 17° when it is separating.

The Moon has an orb of 8° when applying and 12° when separating. Other planets have orbs of 6° and 8°, when applying and separating.

Planets close to the Sun become combust or powerless. This effect of the Sun extends upto 15° and as a planet comes within this distance, it becomes combust and powerless, the full effect of the Sun to "consume" a planet occurring at rapt conjuction when the planet is in the same degree and minute as the Sun. Mercury never becomes combust.

The study and classification of the aspects have developed during the past few decades in the west. There the aspects have been classified as:

Beneficial: Trine, Sextile, Semi-Sextile, Quintile, Semi Quintile and Biquintile.

Adverse or Discordant: Square, Opposition, Semi-Square and Sesqui-Square.

Variable: conjunction and inconjunct.

In general all aspects formed at distances which are multiples of $22\frac{1}{2}^0$ are said to be adverse and all multiples of 18^0 (except 90^0—Square aspect) are favourable.

Western astrologers draw in many cases remarkably accurate conclusions from a detailed study of aspects. Their system is more accurate and scientific than the Indian System which we will now discuss.

Astrologers in India believe that all signs aspect other signs by the opposition aspect, square aspect, trine aspect and some other minor aspects to which we will make brief references later in this chapter. Thus, if a planet be in Cancer for instance, it will be said to be in opposition to planets in Capricorn, irrespective of the angular distance between them. Thus,a planet in the 3rd degree of Cancer will be said to be in opposition to another not only in the 3rd degree of Capricorn but also if it is in the 11th or the 20th or even in the 29^0 of Capricorn. Similarly, with trines or squares, the aspect being counted from sign to sign.

Conjunction, trine, opposition etc., are considered favourable or otherwise not by virtue of the distances involved (in degrees and minutes) but by virtue of whether they are benefics or otherwise, whether they are placed in friendly signs, whether they are inimical or not, whether exalted or debilitated and so on. Indians take the nature of the planets, as determined by the above factors, to determine the good and bad effects to be produced by the aspects they cast. They also believe that planets have a three-fourth and a quarter aspect.

Some special aspects in Indian astrology might be referred to here. Jupiter, apart from the conjunction and opposition aspects forms two special aspects, the 5th and the 9th, that is it aspects strongly the signs fifth and ninth from the sign it occupies. These special aspects are said to be even more powerful and effective than conjunction and opposition. Both are powerful for good, that is for producing beneficial results.

Mars also forms two special aspects, the 4th and the 8th. As Mars generally is considered to be evil, these special aspects are rarely good in terms of the results produced.

Saturn too has two special aspects—the 3rd and the 10th, produced when planets are accupying positions in the 3rd and 10th signs counted from the sign it occupies. These special aspects may or may not produce good results which can be determined by a detailed study of Saturn—its nature, its sign placement, its house placement, its friendliness or otherwise to the aspected planet and so on.

The aspects of all other planets including Rahu and Ketu (Dragon's Head and Tail) that are given a place in Indian Astrology are conjunction and opposition. Indian astrologers had no knowledge of other aspects as listed earlier in this chapter.

While the western aspects must be given a place in modern day astrological practice, my own experience is that the special aspects of Jupiter, Mars and Saturn are important and do produce a clearer understanding of charts that come up for scrutiny. An example may be taken of the 3rd aspect of Saturn which it casts on planets 60^0 (more or less) away from it, i.e., planets in the 3rd sign from the sign it occupies. If Moon is so located in respect of Saturn, then it is subject to the 3rd aspect of Saturn and the result will be generally a worrying mind, with or without cause.

THE NATURE OF THE SIGNS

As mentioned is an earlier chapter, the Zodiac is divided into 12 equal parts, each of 30 degrees, starting from the First Point of Aries and the twelve signs in their serial order are :-

Aries	Libra
Taurus	Scorpio
Gemini	Sagittarius
Cancer	Capricorn
Leo	Aquarius
Virgo	Pisces

They are always shown in the above order whichever be the style in which we draw up the map or the horoscopic chart. In the western and north Indian systems, they are placed anticlockwise in the map while in the south Indian system they appear clockwise, but always in their serial order. The signs were visualised by the ancient observers of the heavens as under:

Aries was the Ram, as the stars forming it appear like the horns of a Ram. It also has some of the qualities of the Ram, an aggressive fighter, full of vigour and energy. Its ruler is Mars which has similar qualities.

Taurus contains stars shaped like the big horns of a Bull when it is observed in the heavens. It has similar qualities, stolid and patient but aggressive like a bull when aroused. It is ruled by Venus.

Gemini is the Twins (or in the Indian version the sexual couple), two distinct figures being visible in the corresponding portion of the sky. Its double nature is appropriately connected with Mercury which has rulership over it.

Cancer is the Crab ruled by the Moon.

Leo shaped like the majestic Lion is the 5th sign, ruled by the Sun.

Virgo is the Virgin or, in the Indian version the Maiden, ruled by Mercury, which when placed in it is said to be exalted.

Libra is represented as the Scales or the Balance, in both the Western and the Indian systems and is ruled by Venus.

Scorpio which in the heavens is a beautiful constellation of stars extending, for northern observers, deep into the southern skies as it is a sign occupied by the Sun at the beginning of winter in November-December. It is ruled by Mars.

Sagittarius the Archer, half animal, half human is ruled by Jupiter and in the Indian System the Sun occupies Sagittarius from the 15th December to the 14th January every year.

Capricorn is visualised as the Crocodile and is ruled by Saturn which also rules the next sign *Aquarius* visualised as a man with a water pot on his shoulder.

The last sign extending from 330^0 to 360^0 when counted from 0^0 Aries, is *Pisces* or the two Fishes, ruled by Jupiter.

The signs have many qualities which one must bear in mind when reading a chart. These are summarised below:

I. The first classification is into Fiery, Earthy, Airy and Watery signs. The *Fiery* signs are Aries, Leo and Sagittarius and the planets in these signs are said to be more active than in others for these signs show such characteristics as enthusiasm, assertion, vigour, courage, pushfulness, enterprise, desire to be in command in any situation and argumentativeness. Appropriately, the rulers of these signs are Mars, Sun, and Jupiter; all planets showing fiery nature, command, enterprise and much energy.

Earthy signs are Taurus, Virgo and Capricorn and show material-mindedness, stability, solidity, caution, prudence, methodical, plodding, slow and practical. Such natives (with earthy signs rising) are not much inclined for flights of fancy; they do not build castles in the air and in every situation will be firmly rooted to the earth or to reality. Imagination will not lead them astray. They will be normally business minded, business dealing with groceries, food and beverages, land, agriculture, building material and even timber naturally attracts them.

The practising astrologer must bear in mind that every situation involves a blend of many astrological forces. For instance, if an earth bound sign such as Taurus or Virgo is in the ascendant or the 10th house (10th being closely connected to one's profession) but if Sun is in a fiery sign and Moon is in an airy sign, such a configuration will alter the characteristics in a major way. The astrologer must always blend the various forces and as he acquires experience, he will be able to read charts more and more correctly, by a proper blend of the factors involved.

Airy signs are Gemini, Libra and Aquarius. Here though vitality is not so robust as in earthy signs, one's mental qualities are well marked. Persons in whose charts airy signs are dominant are cheerful and humorous, imaginative, well-informed and they like professions where brain work and braininess is involved. Artistic or literary professions, journalism, accountancy, communication, good judgement all come naturally to them. They indulge in flights of fancy and love variety. They feel uncomfortable when required to stick to an unchanging and fixed situation where their minds cannot play around. They are humane and cannot tolerate cruelty towards others or even towards animals.

Watery signs are Cancer, Scorpio and Pisces. I might mention here that Cancer (movable sign) is connected to rivers, Scorpio (a fixed sign) to tanks and lakes and Pisces to the oceans. Thus, all are watery signs but differ from one another in this respect.

While watery signs show much emotion, they also indicate lack of action or energy. It is as if the fire of the fiery signs is extinquished in the watery sign. They do not want to go out and act or do something positive. In a group they will be a bit timid and shy leaving it to the persons of fiery signs to lead.

They like occupations connected with liquids, wines and spirits, mineral water as well as with sailing, ship-building, fishing, bottled goods or drinks. Their emotional and psychic nature is strong. They are receptive and therefore, they absorb quickly and take on the idioms and mannerisms of the people they are put in contact with over prolonged periods of time. They are also inclined, more than persons born under other signs, to such ailments as throat and chest troubles, T.B., tumours and cancer.

II. Movable, Fixed and Common signs. Each of these groups contain four signs. The movable signs are Aries, Cancer, Libra and Capricorn and show independence, spirited attitude, pioneering nature and prominence as well as some restlessness.

The fixed signs are Taurus, Leo, Scorpio and Aquarius and as I have observed earlier in connection with Taurus, they show solidity and even stolidity, stubbornness and much patience. They lack the versatility of the airy sign and frequently appear to be of "one track" mind, fixed in their opinions and their actions in a well determined track. This also increases their reliability and makes for lasting friendship. They love luxury and comforts. As they continue for long in their chosen track, they normally succeed and earn much wealth.

The Mutable and Common signs are Gemini, Virgo, Sagittarius and Pisces. They give versatility, love of detail, vacillation and such natives frequently fail because they do not stick to one thing for long and may even leave things unfinished. It is as if they get bored with one and the same profession or person and their love of change makes them start something new, whether it is their profession or their girl or boy friend. Variety is the spice of life, they feel and their love of variety can find free play in professions such as journalism, trade, sports and so on.

Other classification of the signs are :-

III. Positive and Negative. Signs are classified alternatively as positive and negative beginning with Aries which is positive.

IV. Fruitful and barren signs. All the watery signs (Cancer, Scorpio and Pisces) are fruitful so also Aquarius. Taurus, Libra, Sagittarius and Capricorn are semi-fruitful. Aries, Gemini, Leo and Virgo are said to be barren.

V. Violent signs are Aries and Scorpio.

VI. Mute Signs—the watery signs are Mute signs—Cancer, Scorpio and Pisces.

VII. Voice signs are the airy signs of Gemini, Libra and Aquarius.

VIII. Bestial signs are Aries (the Ram), Taurus (the Bull), Leo (the Lion) and Capricorn (the crocodile). The second half of Sagittarius will also come in this class as Sagittarius has the upper or first half shaped like an archer but the lower half is visualised as a quadruped.

IX. Dual signs are Gemini, Sagittarius and Pisces as they are visualised respectively as the Twins, the Archer with the trunk and legs of an animal and Pisces (two fishes).

X. Human signs are Gemini, Virgo, Aquarius and the first half of Sagittarius all picturised with human form.

XI. Double bodied signs—Gemini, first half of Sagittarius and Pisces.

XII. Signs of long ascension are Cancer, Leo, Virgo, Libra, Scorpio and Sagittarius and are so called because of the longer time they take in ascending. This is the case only in northern hemisphere. The other six signs are of short ascension. In the southern hemisphere this classification will be reversed.

XIII. Northern and Southern signs. The first six signs—Aries, Taurus, Gemini, Cancer, Leo and Virgo are the northern signs. The others are southern signs. Moon and other planets for instance when located in the southern signs appear to us as located far in the southern sky, particularly in the easily identified winter signs of Scorpio and Sagittarius.

In discussing this classification, it is perhaps necessary to say the most important are the first (Fiery, airy, earthy, and watery signs) and the second (Movable, Fixed and Common signs). It is these two classes which have been discussed above in some detail. The other classifications are not of great importance. Also their names make it clear what they are about and no elaboration is necessary.

Signs rise in the eastern horizon by virtue of the axial rotation of the earth, every sign taking about two hours. This is easy to understand as the twelve signs have to rise, one after the other, every twenty four hours. The slight difference in the time taken is due to the angle they form with respect to the latitude of the place of observation, north or south of the equator.

Some other pecularities of the above classification may also be noted here. Every quarter of the zodiac begins with fiery sign. Fire and Air are friends and so also are water and earth. A Fire sign is always opposite an Air sign in the map that the astrologer draws up and a Water sign is always opposite an Earthy sign.

Due to the precession of the equinoxes, the difference between the stellar or fixed zodiac and the moving or tropical zodiac followed in the western system in increasing every year. It has been calculated that this precession takes 26,000 years to complete a full circle. It is always moving in a reverse direction—from Aries to Pisces to Aquarius and so on. In this book as I have also mentioned earlier, the fixed or sidereal zodiac has been followed. It begins at the point or degree occupied by the sun on the 13th April every year and the sign Aries is occupied by the sun from the 13th April to the 14th May, and not from the 21st March to the 20th April as in the Tropical system. The reader of any astrological work or article must always be quite clear about the system allowed in that work or article so that he does not get confused by various observations in it.

Signs Versus Houses

Beginners are apt to get confused when dealing with signs and houses. It is therefore necessary to understand clearly what exactly they are and how they differ from one another.

A sign is a 30^0 division of the ecliptic beginning from a definite and unvarying point. Thus, there are 12 Signs in the 360^0 forming the circle of the ecliptic. The signs are Aries, Taurus, Gemini, Cancer, Leo, Virgo, Libra, Scorpio, Sagittarius, Capricorn, Aquarius and Pisces, each of which is given a well defined character. Signs arise in the East as the earth rotates on its axis from West to East. The earth is nearly spherical but the axis of the earth is inclined in respect to the Equator, this inclination being 23^0 27'. It is this inclination that causes summer and winter and it is due to it that some signs appear to be far to the north of the equator and some to the south.

The Earth moves at about 18½ miles or 30 Kilometres per second in its journey around the Sun. As we also move along with the earth, we are not aware of its motion. The Sun too moves at a speed of about 250 miles per second in its journey in the Milky Way. The Milky Way itself is in motion—so are all other Nebulae. For two bodies moving along in parrallel paths, one will not be conscious of motion. It is only when motion is not at the same speed or velocity and when there is an angular velocity that we become aware of motion. On Earth however, everything stays put as it were for the observer and for him therefore there is no motion.

We start counting the signs from the first degree of Aries onwards to the last degree of Pisces. The Sun enters Aries on the 21st March according to the Moving Zodiac and on the 13th April if we follow the Sidereal Zodiac. The other signs in which the Sun is located are as under.

	Tropical Zodiac	*Sidereal Zodiac*
Taurus	Apr. 21 to May 20	May 14 to June 15
Gemini	May 21 to June 20	June 15 to July 16
Cancer	June 21 to July 21	July 16 to Aug. 16
Leo	July 22 to Aug. 21	Aug. 16 to Sept. 16
Virgo	Aug. 22 to Sept. 21	Sept. 16 to Oct. 16
Libra	Sept. 22 to Oct. 22	Oct. 16 to Nov. 15
Scorpio	Oct. 23 to Nov. 21	Nov. 15 to Dec. 15
Sagittarius	Nov. 22 to Dec. 20	Dec. 15 to Jan. 14
Capricorn	Dec. 21 to Jan. 19	Jan. 14 to Feb. 13
Aquarius	Jan. 20 to Feb. 18	Feb. 13 to Mar. 15
Pisces	Feb. 19 to Mar. 20	Mar. 15 to Apr. 13

These dates are relevent when readings of one's chart on the basis of only the Sun signs are being made, as in the newspapers and magazines.

When we come to *Houses* it must be borne in mind that while there are 12 houses, each approximately of 30^0 extension (this varies with different systems of house divisions such as Placidus, Campanus etc.) any sign can be located in any house. Houses are counted from the first or ascendant, i.e., the degree of the Zodiac arising on the Eastern Horizon at the moment of birth. This first house or ascendant will extend to the degree 30^0 beyond the ascending degree. (For the purpose of this book we will proceed on the basis of the equal house division). Thus, if, say, the 18th degree of Cancer is rising, the first house will extend to 17th degree of the next sign Leo. The second house will be from the 18th degree of Leo to the 17th degree of Virgo and so on for the 3rd, 4th and all subsequent houses upto the 12th or the last house. While signs are numbered and counted from Aries, houses are counted and numbered from the *ascendant*. While Aries is the first sign, the first house may have Aries in it or Taurus or Libra or Pisces depending on whether it was Aries that was rising in the Eastern horizon or Taurus or Libra or Pisces. Similarly the 5th house may or may not have the 5th sign Leo in it. The 10th may or may not have any connection with Capricorn, the 10th Sign.

In the natal chart houses are numbered 1, 2, 3 and so on and these numbers should never be confused with the signs given numbers 1, 2, 3 and so on for Aries, Taurus, Gemini etc. The reader must always remember this.

Another important point that the reader has to bear in mind when dealing with Indian charts is connected with the Moon sign. Indians attach great importance to the Moon sign—even more than to the Sun sign—so much so that the Moon sign is called by its own name, the Rashi. When examining charts, the first thing an astrologer does is to examine the Rashi. Here again one must bear in mind that the Moon at birth can be in any of the 12 houses. The sign positions will give us the Rashi in which one is born and the astrologer will normally commence his analysis with this Rashi.

If one says my Rashi is Virgo it means that one was born when Moon was in Virgo. This Rashi position will frequently decide his name—beginning with P as I have mentioned in an earlier chapter. The Rashi is no less important than the ascendant or the Sun sign. Here I might say that the Indian analyst gives most importance to the Rashi, next to the ascendant and last to the Sun sign, whereas most western astrologers will begin with the Sun sign and only thereafter come to the ascendant and the Moon sign in that order. The main reason for the importance given to the Moon sign is that Moon controls or governs the mind; it has much to do with the survival of the child, a weak Moon receiving adverse aspects, say, from the second house often acting against his or her chances of survival. This is also the case if Moon is located in the 6th house and is weak, i.e., close to its New Moon position.

Having understood clearly what a house is and how it is related to signs, we can now proceed to examine the Houses and Signs in more detail.

THE SIGNS

The twelve signs into which the ecliptic and the zodiac have been divided, have been recognised since ancient times. The signs are all of 30^0 and form a vast circle in the heavens. The Sun and all the planets go round this circle and spend varying periods in each of the signs. It is normal to begin with the sign Aries because the vernal equinox takes place when the sun enters Aries.

Aries

This is the first sign of the zodiac extending from 0^0 to 30^0 along the ecliptic. The sun is in Aries from the 13th April to the 14th May. In the Sidereal system the exact moment at which the sun enters a sign is taken into account because many Hindu festivals are connected with the time of the solar entry into signs. This moment is frequently after midnight and hence the date on which one sign ends and the next begins are both given in the Indian almanacs. Thus, the Sun entered Gemini on June 15th at 8.02 a.m. in 1994. It will, therefore, be correct to say that Gemini began on June 15th (and thus Taurus ended also on June 15, in the morning). So also for the other signs.

Aries is a fiery sign, movable and barren. It is violent and bestial. It is a positive and masculine sign and hot by nature and is appropriately ruled by Mars. It is the head of *Kalapurusha*. Sun is exalted in this sign, the exact degree of exaltation being 10^0. Thus for all persons born on the 22nd or 23rd April, Sun is fully exalted. If it is also well placed by its house position, it will be of great benefit to the native.

Saturn gets debilitated in Aries. The Hindus say that Saturn is the son of Sun and is a bitter enemy of the Sun. It is quite appropriate, therefore, to say that when the Sun is happy (in Aries), Saturn is unhappy and can therefore cause some harmful effects from its debilitated position.

Venus is the ruler of Libra. As Aries is the 7th sign from Libra, Venus is said to be in its fall when located in Aries. Even otherwise Venus is not happy in the sign of Mars which is ascribed qualities quite different and even opposite of those given to Venus.

Aries when rising shows activity, boldness, even a headstrong nature, great self-confidence, ability to lead and be a pioneer. It is difficult to keep Arians in their place since they will attempt to usurp a position not strictly theirs if given the slightest indulgence.

One profession in which Arians are largely found is the police, far in excess of what is determined strictly by the law of averages. The policeman has to be more or less fearless, active, sometimes using violence even if it be only his baton or truncheon. He enjoys aggression when sanctioned by the laws of his land and charges into a crowd, hitting out to the left and right.

Arians are generally egoistic and even boastful. For them achieving thier ends is most important whatever be the means followed.

Many women fall for their frank and dominating nature. Aries women are extremely jealous and can throw a fit if their husband makes the mistake of praising another woman in their presence. Otherwise they like to look up to their men. They keep a good home but may spend more than they earn, running into debts.

Aries, being the first of all twelve signs, it is said to be the natural ruler of the first house. As any of the twelve signs can fall into the first house or ascendant, it will be said that while Mars is the natural ruler of the first house, the planet owning the corresponding sign will be the accidental ruler of the first house. In practice however, one should give due importance to the sign ruler and only thereafter to the natural ruler.

The sounds allotted to Aries are Ch, L and A. The Nakshatras it contains are—Ashwini, Bharani and first quarter of Krittika, ruled respectively by Ketu, Venus and Sun. This is important when working out the *dashas*.

Taurus

This sign is symbolised by the Bull and extends from 30^0 to 60^0 along the ecliptic. It is fixed, feminine and earthy. It rules the mouth and cheeks. Its sounds are E,A,O and V. Sun is in this sign from May 14 to June 15. Taurus natives have many of the qualities of the Bull, not easily aroused but when they are aroused they rush headlong into attack. They are plodding, persevering and of strong will. Their opinions are fixed and it takes long experience to change them whereas a more imaginative and less obstinate person can see early that a certain opinion or course of action is not in accordance with the situation or with reality and is quick to change it.

As enemies they are relentless and when dealing with Taureans one must be cautious and never infuriate them. One has to be patient with them as it takes much persuasion and tact to change their opinions.

Taureans love the pleasures of the table. It is perhaps with Taureans in mind that one has said that the way to their hearts is through their stomach. Wives of Taureans should therefore learn to please them through good food.

Taurus rules the throat and neck which are the weak parts in an otherwise robust and strong body, thick set and with a big and full mouth.

Venus is the ruler of this sign and while no planet is debilitated in Taurus, Moon becomes exalted when located in it. The Nakshatra most loved by Moon (of the three it rules) is located in Taurus. It is Rohini and when Moon is in Rohini, Moon dasha is operative, its full period being 10 years.

Venus being the ruler of the sign, Taureans will go for Venusian professions such as those involving luxury goods, money, agriculture, cooking and art or decoration.

Gemini

Gemini, the third sign of the zodiac extends from 60^0 to 90^0. It is an airy sign and is mutable. The sun resides in Gemini from the 15th June to 16th July every year. No planet gets exalted or debilitated in Gemini.

Gemini is a dual sign. Its colour is said to be green, like that of a parrot. It rules over the arms and shoulders as well as the lungs and nerves. Its sounds are K, Gha, and H (as in Ha!).

The Nakshatras it rules are Mrigashira second half, Ardra and 3/4th of Punarvasu.

Mercury rules over Gemini. Quite appropriately so, for Mercury also has governance over quick wit, intelligence, humour. Gemini borns will live mainly in an intellectual world, the higher types being attracted towards public speaking, diplomacy and literary or journalistic lines. The lower types will go for book keeping, salesmen or as clerks.

If we remember that Gemini borns live mostly in the mind, we will be able to undestand their inconsistency and the tendency to begin something with great enthusiasm but to get bored with it quite soon. Thus, they lack the fixity of purpose and long continued effort so necessary to bring success in most lines. This love of variety develops in them a peculiar charm as they can talk with much eloquence on any subject and women/girls fall for them because they concentrate their minds and emotions for a short while and thus charm their listeners. However, their love for variety will soon make them turn away, to someone else or to some other subject. Their wives should not expect constancy from them. At the same time, jealousy will also be out of place because Gemini borns will be attracted only for a short while, without any desire to form a permanent bond. Gemini wives will also have an intellectual atmosphere around them. They will be quick to complete all duties connected to housekeeping or running a home and thereafter they will want to have some work outside the home. They make excellent secretaries, personal assistants, sales-girls, typists as well as journalists, reporters, photographers etc.

It is said of Gemini borns that they are all things to all persons, such is their versatality but they will essentially be a jack of all trades and master of none.

That astrological influences are important in our lives could be proved beyond doubt if a study were to be undertaken amongst journalists and press reporters, the majority of whom will be found to have Gemini ascending in their natal chart or Sun will be in Gemini or Moon will be in Gemini. Readers of this book could try to confirm this by checking on the birth dates of their friends and aquaintances.

Cancer

Cancer is the fourth sign of the Zodiac extending from 90^0 to 120^0 of the ecliptic. It is a watery sign, movable and fruitful and astrologers normally advise farmers to plant when moon is in Cancer not because Cancer is the sign ruled by moon but because it is a fruitful sign. The Nakshatras contained in Cancer are Punarvasu, last quarter, Pushyami and Aslesha, thus completing the first cycle of nine nakshatras, beginning with Aswini and ending with Aslesha.

The sounds allotted to Cancer are H (as in Hay) and D. Cancer is a feminine sign and governs the northern direction. It is an active sign but modest and shy though indicating steady effort. It is also a mute sign and it has been said by some astrologers that if Ketu is located in Cancer in the second house which governs speech, one is inclined to dumbness. If the second house has Cancer in it, some defect in speech (e.g., stuttering) is also frequently associated with the other malefic, Rahu, located in the 2nd house, whichever be the sign occupied by it.

The great benefic Jupiter is exalted when in Cancer but Mars in Cancer is debilitated. As Cancer rules over the breast and lungs, Mars in Cancer is associated with troubles in the chest and lungs, such as pleurisy, pneumonia and even T.B. and asthma. Injuries in the region of the chest and boils are also associated with Mars in Cancer.

However, Jupiter's location in Cancer will cause all kinds of good fortunes to the Cancer borns—good health, good finances, clear mind, truthfulness, goodwill towards others and so on. Nothing evil can befall a person with Jupiter in Cancer, particularly if Cancer be the ascendant. The highest point of exaltation is 5^0 of Cancer.

Cancer is pictured as the Crab and this can also be observed from the way Cancer borns walk clumsily and somewhat with sideways movement of their legs or arms.

As also said earlier, Cancer borns quickly absorb outside influences and just as water takes on the colour of the sky—blue if there is bright sunshine and blue sky and grey or leaden when it becomes cloudy—so also the Cancer borns will pick up the language, intonation, accent and mannerisms of the group in which he or she is placed.

One characteristic of the Cancer borns is that the upper part of the body is larger than the lower and this makes it possible to identify them even from a distance. Their walk thus becomes even more ungainly, particularly in women. Cancer born women, however, can make good housewives and house-keepers too in hotels, as bar-maids and in other occupations connected with liquids.

Cancer borns have strong attachments to the home. They love to operate from the home and to keep all kind of gadgets in their kitchens. They do not easily throw things away even when such things are no longer of any use. They are attracted to service in stores, groceries, restaurants and in hospitals. They can also make good mediums and clairvoyants.

Sun is in Cancer from the 16th July to the 16th August every year.

Leo

The sign Leo extends from 120° to 150° and a new cycle of the nakshatras starts with this sign. The nakshatras are Magha (ruled by Ketu), Purvaphalguni (ruled by Venus) and the first quarter of Uttaraphalguni (ruled by Sun). Leo is a fiery sign and a fixed one, bestial and barren, ruled by the Sun. No planet gets exalted or debilitated in Leo. Its ruler is the Sun.

Sun is in Leo from the 16th of August to the 16th of September every year. The sounds given to Leo are G (as in goat), M and T.

Leo is a masculine sign, fixed, fiery in nature and it governs the direction East. It is symbolised as the Lion and has many of the qualities associated with the Lion, majesty, nobility of character, proud and born leaders and commanders. They are easily influenced by flattery and grant boons freely as it were, when warmed or softened by flattery. They have a strong sense of ego but they are normally not capable of mean actions. They lack the "Mean Gene" of born criminals. Whenever necessary they will take command of the situation and have the ability to shoulder responsibility. Leonians should be chosen as chiefs of divisions, as managers and as foremen for they have the instinct to guide and lead others. Manual work and physical labour are not to their liking.

Owing to their own lofty nature, Leonians are apt to forget that others may be cunning and even mean. Leonians are thus often taken advantage of by others. Suspicion and caution should therefore be learned by Leonians. They must realise that it is not everyone who can be trusted. Leonians may for instance entrust money to others. Some of these others will run away with it, leaving the Leo born wondering how someone could do such a mean thing. Leo is ruled by Sun which is free, generous and frank by nature. Saturn is said to be the son of Sun and has the opposite qualities of caution, suspicion, slowness in action. Therefore Leo borns should learn from Saturn, the son and enemy of Sun and take on some of the desirable qualities of Saturn so that in life they are not cheated or exploited by others.

The eyesight of Leo borns is often affected if malefics occupy the second and twelfth houses or if Sun is adversely aspected.

Virgo

This sixth sign of the Zodiac extends from 150^0 to 180^0 and it contains the nakshatras of Uttaraphalguni (¾th) Hasta and Chitra ½). It is an earthy and common sign. It is ruled by Mercury which also gets exalted in it but Venus in Virgo is debilitated. Sun is in Virgo from Sept.16 to Oct. 16. Its sounds are P and Th.

Virgoans are generally reserved, discriminative and shrewd. They are nervous and hesitant so that frequently they regret that they let the opportunity go when it had presented itself. In the classroom Virgoans will normally ask their Arian colleagues to get up and ask the teacher or professor because the Virgoan will feel too shy to do so himself. In later life also the Virgoan will be hesitating and will keep mum in many situations in which he should really have said some thing. Thus he may be left behind. It is this characteristic of the Virgoans which makes people conclude that the Virgoan is best suited to serve and not to lead.

Virgo rules the intestinal and digestive system. Adverse planets like Mars can lead to stomach upsets. Mars in particular often causes hernia and so operations. Stomach ulcers can also be ascribed to Mars in Virgo.

Virgoans are fond of detail and when expounding something they go into great and frequently unnecessary detail to the extent of boring others. They are quick to find fault in others and often pick them to the threads. This is particularly true of women who will be very critical of other women—their clothes, their mannerisms, their habits. Talkativeness is their weakness.

Virgoans are normally hard working and they expect others too to work hard. When in charge of others they may be a bit too exacting, quick to notice faults or weaknesses of others.

As Virgo is the 6th house of the zodiac, it has much to do with health. Adverse planets in Virgo are a signal of ill health in the dasha of the planet occupying it. A smooth life free of tension amongst beautiful and pollution free surroundings and a diet with plenty of fresh fruits and vegetables will keep them healthy and fit till an advanced age. Excess of alcohol should be avoided by Virgoans. They should learn to relax their minds and bodies and never get too involved with money-making or with the mad race to "get to the top." Otherwise they will ruin their health.

Virgoans frequently run partnership businesses which have double names such as Mark & Spencer, Roy & James, Gaindamal Hansraj, etc.

Libra

The sun is in Libra from Oct.16 to Nov.15 very year. Libra is an airy and movable sign. Its sounds are Ra and Ta (as pronounced in French). The nakshatras ruled by Libra are Chitra (second half), Swati and Vishaka 3/4. Libra extends from 180^0 to 210^0 along the ecliptic. Libra is ruled byVenus and Saturn gets exalted in it. Appropriately its enemy the Sun is debilitated in Libra—another example of the Sun and Saturn never seeing eye to eye.

The Signs

As Libra is the Balance or the Scales, Librans are good judges of all types of situations. They instinctively perceive the factual position in a situation. They are deeply emotional but as they are even-handed, composed, cool and level-headed, others are unable to penetrate their mask. They are pleasant looking and this makes it difficult for others to realise that many Librans are lascivious and pleasure-seeking inside. Both men and women born in Libra are capable of giving much pleasure to their partner.

Libra rules the part of the body just below the navel and the kidneys in particular.

Their love nature is strong but they are frank and sincere. They like to dress well and normally their taste is impeccable. They make good designers in many fields of fashion. As they are courteous, soft spoken and meet others with a smile, they do not make enemies. They have few children, to whom they are deeply attached. Librans are attached to Martian types of partners who may frequently be aggressive and selfish and strongly sexed. Much caution is, therefore, necessary in choosing friends of the opposite sex. The colour orange and soft reds are in harmony with their nature.

As Venus is also the lord of the 8th house for those born in Libra (Libra ascendant), they may have to face occasions where their self-respect is threatened. They meet with unwarranted insults generally caused by or connected with their sexual partners. The number 7 will be lucky for them and also Tuesdays and Saturdays.

Librans can be recognised from their humid feet which begin to smell unpleasantly unless they are washed and kept clean.

Scorpio

This eighth sign of the zodiac extends from 210 degrees to 240 degrees along the ecliptic. It is governed by the fiery Mars —though Scorpio is a watery sign but fixed in quality. Sun is in Scorpio from Nov.15 to Dec.15 every year. The nakshatras in Scorpio are Vishaka (1/4), Anuradha and Jyestha. It has rulership over the sounds N and Y (Na and Ya). The sexual organs and the anus of *Kalapurusha* are located in this sign. It is symbolised as the Scorpion. It is a southern sign and easily identifiable in the southern skies at night.

Scorpio, whatever be its weaknesses is a powerful sign—strong, determined, shrewd and secretive, so much so that Scorpio borns are said to make the best detectives, spies and intelligent men. They will not permit others to take any liberties with them, even though their magnetic nature attracts others towards them.

They have deep and unfathomable eyes. Scorpio being the sign governing sexual organs they are normally strongly sexed, coming to the act without much foreplay or imagination or emotions, thus causing their partners to feel unsatisfied and even resentful. They can descend to the depths of debauchery. Moon in Scorpio will give them a tongue vicious as the sting of a scorpion with the result that they make many enemies. The polish and soft spoken nature of the Libran will be completely absent in Scorpio borns.

Jealousy and intolerance are strong traits. Normally they can brook no opposition, they do not forgive easily, are dogmatic and suspicious but capable of much achievement where their love of mastery is allowed free play. They make good surgeons and military men as well as butchers. (Napolean is said to have been born when Scorpio was rising).

As lord of the ascendant is also the lord of the 6th house (of enemies), the fact that they make many enemies should cause no surprise.

Many wife-beaters, shrews and women who hit their husbands will fall in this sign and also many drug takers.

Sagittarius

This is a sign in which Sun has residence from 15th December to the 14th January every year. Though a winter sign for people in the northern hemisphere, it is a fiery sign of mutable quality and is ruled by the great benefic Jupiter which makes Sagittarians cheerful, optimistic and great lovers of sports. The sign starts the third and last cycle of the nine nakshatras and contains Moola ruled by Ketu, Purvashada ruled by Venus and the first quarter of Uttarashada, ruled by Sun. It extends from 240^0 to 270^0 along the ecliptic. No planet is exalted or debilitated in Sagittarius. It governs the sounds Yay, Bha and Pha. It is a masculine sign, ruling the eastern direction and it contains the thigh of *Kala Purusha*.

Jupiter is a born teacher and guide for others and Hindus consider that he is the Guru of the Gods, so much so that Jupiter is called Guru. Sagittarians will therefore have the quality of gathering people around them to guide them along the path to self-realisation. They are basically just persons and are inwardly so honest that others come to trust them. They are unhappy when solitary and love to mix with others and spend their time in a group. A marked short-coming in them is the lack of tact and often they blurt out something a tactful person would never say in a group.

They make good professors, engineers, sports persons and usually succeed in their chosen line. They are fond of pets and the company of the opposite sex. They may suffer from sciatica gout or rheumatism in later life. Sagittarian wives give very good advice to their husbands, are tactful and understanding and know when to be silent. Yet, Sagittarians do not get as good a home life as they expect.

Capricorn

It is ruled by Saturn and is pictured as the alligator. It is a movable sign but earthy in nature. Sun is in Capricorn from the 14th January to the 13th of February. It contains the Nakshatras of Uttarashada (3/4), Sravana and half of

Dhanishta. It governs the sound J, Kh and Ga (as in gate). It is a feminine sign and governs the southern direction. The knees of *Kala Purusha* are located in this sign.

Capricorn gives a plodding nature, practical and shrewd. They abhor wastefulness in any form and are just but hard. Sagittarians are also basically lovers of justice but whereas a Sagittarian will forgive and forget an act of injustice, a Capricornian will insist on his pound of flesh and will remember it for years.

Capricornians are hardworking and often do very well in financial circles. They have a sacrificial nature and are ambitious.

Mars gets exalted in Capricorn but Jupiter in Capricorn is debilitated. As the sign is ruled by Saturn, Capricornians do not show a sociable and humourous face to their children but are inclined to be stern with them, teaching them the virtue of long and patient work.

Aquarius

This is the second sign ruled by Saturn. It extends from 300^0 to 330^0 along the ecliptic. Sun remains in Aquarius from the 13th February to March 15th. It governs the sound Sa, Si, Da and G (as in good and gold).

Aquarius is an airy sign and is fixed. It contains the nakshatras of Dhanishta (second half), Satabhisha and Purvabhadrapada (3/4th). Aquarius contains the ankles and the lower part of the legs of *Kala Purusha* and these are the parts that are easily affected when adversly aspected or in adverse houses.

Aquarians are original persons and make good and life-long friends. It is felt by many western astrologers that rulership of this sign should be given to Uranus, a planet that was unknown in ancient times when astrology was born.

Aquarius is symbolised as a man bearing a pot of water on his shoulder. At some time in their life they feel attracted to ascetism. Normally, however, they are cheerful people enjoying social contacts and friendships. However, if they come to feel that their partners are not upto the mark, they will quietly and without fuss or quarrels proceed to change them.

Pisces

This last sign of the zodiac extends from 330° to 360° and plays host to the Sun from the 15th March to the 13th April every year. It contains the nakshatras of Purvabhadrapada (1/4) Uttarabhadrapada and Revati. It is a watery sign and of mutable quality. It forms the feet of *Kala Purusha* and its sounds are D (as pronounced in French) and Cha. It is a feminine sign and owns the Northern direction. While Venus gets exalted in Pisces, Mercury gets debilitated. Jupiter owns Pisces, though some astrologers are inclined to allot Neptune ownership of the sign.

Pisces is a sign which shows kindness, is mild in nature and charitable but its sensitiveness makes Pisceans (or Piscureans as many prefer to put it) somewhat pessimistic, withdrawn, preferring to stay back lest they get hurt mentally if they try to come forward and take the world by its horns as it were. This tendency to withdraw makes them easy-going and diffident but their love of humanity becomes obvious from the fact that nursing, charity and aid giving organisations attract them when they are choosing a profession.

They are also attracted by professions connected with the sea. This is not surprising since the sign is symbolised as two fishes facing north and south respectively.

The Houses

The difference between signs and houses has been explained earlier but in view of the confusion that often arises in the mind of the beginner, it might be desirable to explain it over again. While the signs are 30^0 divisions of the zodiacal belt in the heavens beginning with Aries which the Sun enters at the spring equinox, the houses are determined from the degree and sign rising on the eastern horizon at the moment of birth, the first house extending 30^0 from this rising degree, the second from the end of the first house to the next 30^0 point and so on. Thus, if 7^0 Taurus is rising on the eastern horizon, the first house will be 7^0 Taurus to 6^0 Gemini, the second from 7^0 Gemini to 6^0 Cancer and so on till we come to the 12th and the last house which in this case will be from 7^0 Aries to 6^0 Taurus. While Aries is the first sign of the zodiac, in the example just cited, the bulk of it will fall in the 12th house—7^0 Aries to 30^0 Aries as well as the first 6^0 of Taurus falling in the 12th house.

Signs have their own importance and significance. Houses are no less important as will be clear from the following study of the houses.

First House: Shows the basic character of the native, his body and character and the way he or she reacts to things. It is an angular house, the other angular houses being the 4th, 7th and 10th. Hindu astrologers give special importance to the angular houses and benefics in them show much good fortune. If all the four angular houses are occupied by benefics (as was the case in the chart of Dr. Rajendra Prasad, former President of India), this is an exceptionally good indication of fortune, rise in life, dignity and honours and so on. Their importance may also be seen from the belief that even malefics become favourable if they own angular houses.

Jupiter's location in an angle is exceptionally favourable in the Hindu view and is said to ward off all evil influences.

Second House: is the house that governs money matters, jewellery and clothes, speech, the family in general and his or her kith and kin. Rahu and Ketu in the second house adversely affect one's speech, causing speech defects such as stuttering, lisping and even dumbness. The second house is also considered to be a death inflicting house, the other such house being the 7th. The second also governs the second marriage and eyesight.

Third House: governs brothers and sisters, neighbours, short journeys, writing, changes of residence or vocation, sale of house and death of mother. Mars, Rahu, Ketu and Saturn in 3rd indicate that one has no younger brother or else the younger brother dies in the dasha or period of malefics influencing the third house. Many planets in the third and particularly if any of them is also a malefic is a definite and invariable influence for many changes of residence or short travels, so much so that it can be boldly asserted that such an influence is as good as a law of science—it is invariably true. Three or more planets in the third show that one will take to the profession of travelling salesman, or a truck driver, always on the move upto 20 or 25 days in a month. Mars or Rahu in the third show death of younger brother in their dashas as well as changes in location. As the 3rd house also shows courage, if the lord of the ascendant is located in the third, the native will have the power to resist adversity. He will also be found to possess the power to meet challenges. While Mars is generally evil in its influence, if located in the third, it will bestow on the native great power to resist misfortunes.

Fourth House: shows the home, landed or immovable property, mother, happiness and later part of one's life. It is the second angular house and its natural ruler is the Moon, the fourth sign being Cancer ruled by the Moon. The fourth house has also to do with agriculture. As it shows the home, if the 4th lord is in a fixed sign, it shows that one will stay in the same place or location, averse to travel, more so if the 4th is also in a fixed sign. The fourth is also important in the matter of mental peace and a peaceful life in general, for which the influences of evil planets should be absent from the fourth house or its lord.

Fifth House: influences are summed up in three words—creation, procreation and recreation. It is the house showing creative abilities and as I have mentioned in another chapter, Venus in the fifth is a strong indication of creative ability, poetry, painting or any of the fine arts. That it governs procreation shows that the fifth is connected with the children and progeny. Mars and the Sun in the fifth indicate disharmony between the father and son, even to the extent of the son leaving the house after a quarrel with the father.

The fifth is also connected with speculation and lotteries and with politics and politicians but the most important aspect of one's life that it governs is one's sex life and love affairs. Among the earliest societies hunting was important because it was the activity essential to survival. In developed countries today the problem of hunger has been largely taken care of and even unemployed persons are given the dole so that nowadays nobody starves. Modern society thus is swayed by the next most important instinct of sex and how it develops in man is determined by the fifth house. Planets like Venus, Mars and Saturn will invaribly and without exception make one a philanderer if located in the fifth or connected to the fifth by aspects, provided Jupiter does not save the situation by conjunction or other strong beneficial aspects. Similarly Uranus in the fifth shows unconventional sex.

The fifth house is also a trine, the other trine being the ninth. The first house or ascendant is also a trine in addition to being an angular house. All the three trines are important houses more than the other succedent or cadent houses and a proper and detailed study of them is necessary before an astrologer forms an opinion of the natal chart. However, the fifth is important for love affairs and a woman having Saturn and Venus in the fifth will go for anything in pants and men will be skirt chasers.

Sixth House: holds sway over disease, service, enemies, employment and it also stands for the anus. Malefics such as Rahu and Mars in the 6th will make the native develop such diseases as piles and fistula in their dashas or periods, leading often to surgery. Mars in the 6th shows that the native will, by his own action, create enemies and then try, often successfully, to vanquish them. Such a native will often enjoy fights. He should learn to control excessive aggression in his deeds and in speech.

Seventh House: This is the third of the angular houses and holds sway over such departments of life as marriage, partners, break in journey, the spouse and the person or persons one comes across in life for business or social dealings. Malefics in the 7th cause some sort of disharmony in married life. Thus, Saturn in 7th is a factor for delay in marriage and some coldness between the partners.

Mars in the 7th shows an aggressive attitude towards the partner. Moon in such signs as Libra will give one a beautiful wife. The Sun is adverse in the 7th and frequently shows forced separation due to a foreign posting or transfer to a non-family station.

The seventh is considered to be a death-inflicting house. For those born in an ascendant in a common sign, the seventh assumes "killer" properties in its dasha or sub-period. (for movable signs in the ascendant such a property goes to the 11th house and for fixed signs to the ninth). These days the medical sciences have made great progress. Nevertheless, the "killer" houses do cause health problems, though they may not cause death as the doctor will normally save you. Yet, the planets owning such houses and the planets occupying these houses as well as planets in the nakshatras of such planets are important when judging danger to life due to the death inflicting or "killer" tendencies associated with these houses.

Seventh house is also important in connection with diseases of the sexual organs. Ketu in 7th, particularly if conjoined with Mars will lead to operations for hydrocele and such other diseases.

Eighth House: is considered by Hindu astrology to be the worst of the three malefic houses—the 6th, the 8th and the 12th. It has much to do with death. Saturn in this house causes slow death. The native may have a stroke and may continue to be bedridden or even semi-conscious for many weeks or even months before death comes to him. Uranus in the 8th causes death by an accident or electric shock or otherwise a quick and sudden death. Jupiter and Venus in the 8th show that death will be peaceful. Mercury in the 8th indicates that the native will be conscious till the last moment. Mars shows death due to injury or wounds.

Mars in the 8th also shows that the native will spend and even waste the wealth of the spouse. It is adverse for the longevity of the spouse, so much so that many will think twice before agreeing to a marriage with a girl in whose chart Mars is in the 8th house.

The 8th house also shows snubs and insults received by the native. If Venus is in the 8th and particularly if in an unfriendly sign such as Aries, the native will receive insults through or because of women in the dasha or sub-periods of Venus.

Ninth House: is the second and most important trine. Hindus consider it to be the house of good fortune, good deeds, virtue, the father, long journeys including overseas travels, religion and more particularly the higher forms of religion, philosophy, spirituality and also astrology. It is the house one should turn to first, for if it is well located and occupied, this gives the native a great advantage in his struggle for success and good fortune in life. Among the most fortunate configurations in a natal chart are the location of the ascendant lord in the 9th, Jupiter in the 9th, the lord of 10 in the 9th with the 9th lord located in the 10th which forms a special and powerful yoga or combination. This mutual exchange of position of the 9th and 10th lords is powerful enough but even if the 9th and 10th lords are combined in any other house, this too causes the yoga to manifest itself.

Mercury and Jupiter in the 9th are favourable for a study of astrology. Saturn in the 9th is favourable for archaeology and Jupiter for preachers and the religious orders particularly for those born early in the afternoon when Sun is also located in the 9th.

The planet owning or occupying the 9th will in its period or dasha take the native on a long journey. The 9th also rules over writing and publishing of books on some serious subject. Since the second house counted from any house is the natural death inflicting planet for the matters signified by that house and as the 9th house stands for the father, the lord of the 9th if located in the 10th will in its dasha or sub-period indicate death of the father. I have personally come across innumerable cases where the truth of this general rule has been fully vindicated. Planets owning the 9th house of good fortune will be benefic to the native, even though such planets be otherwise evil (such as Mars and Saturn), so important is the 9th in protecting the native in his journey through life.

Tenth House: corresponds to the zenith or mid-heaven and is the fourth of the angles. It governs one's career and wordly position, profession or business and planets located on the midheaven obviously have great strength. As I have also said earlier, if all the angles are occupied by benefics or planets benefic by lordship, this special Yoga is called the yoga of the four oceans and lifts the person to very high wordly position as in the case of the first President of India, Dr. Rajendra Prasad.

Saturn in the 10th indicates obstacles and delay in one's attempts to rise in life. Uranus shows electricity or careers connected with electricity or computers or aviation. Jupiter bestows much dignity and respect as in the case of judges, ambassadors, senators and so on. Mars has connection with the armed forces or engineering and if Mars is not adverse by location or lordship, bestows much energy and honour. Sun in 10th is beneficial for a career in government or civil services. Mercury is good for journalism, writing or other intellectual or secretarial pursuits. Venus indicates cinema, the stage or the arts or such careers as modelling, fashion, dress-making and so on.

Eleventh House: stands primarily for friends and gains. It also has sway over one's vehicle and elder brother.

If a number of planets are located in the eleventh house, this shows one's ability to make friends quickly. Such a person can mix with senators, ministers as well as with workmen and labourers.

The eleventh is also connected with liaisons of a casual nature. Saturn, Uranus or Neptune or Venus in the 11th are sure to cause many casual affairs and temporary liaisons. Such persons seem to attract the opposite sex so strongly that nobody says "no" to them.

The lord of the ascendant when placed in the 11th is a good position for general well-being and gain. The lord of the 2nd house when in the 11th and the lord of the 11th placed in the 2nd which is the house of wealth are sure indications of much wealth coming one's way without much effort. Similarly, planets in the nakshatra owned by a planet located in the 11th house will in their dashas and sub-periods bring continuous gain and wealth to the native.

Planets in the 11th produce such results which are indicated by their nature. Thus, Moon in the 11th will give many friends of a casual nature or friendship not involving much depth and particularly amongst women. Jupiter will give friendship among men in high position. Similarly for the other planets.

Twelfth House: is generally considered to be an evil house as it governs such affairs as loss, seclusion, imprisonment and secret enemies. Mars and the lord of the 3rd are indicative of restraints, injury and suicidal tendencies. Moon in 12th shows dislocation, worries and seclusion. Sun in 12th may lead to confinement in an institution. Venus in 12th shows pleasures with the opposite sex but may ultimately lead to enmity. Mars is said to be a thief and if Mars is located in the 12th without any benefic aspect, will lead to thievish tendencies and shop lifting.

A good horoscope should preferably have no planet in the 12th house. However the lord of the 12th has to be located in some house. As it is to be considered generally evil because of lordship over the 12th, it should preferably be in an adverse house such as 3rd or the 8th or be aspected by Saturn which will render it largely ineffective and powerless to produce 12th house effects.

Some General Principles

I have in the preceding pages dealt with the 12 signs as well as the 12 houses or the 12 mansions of the natal chart. Before we study the planets in some detail, it is necessary to be clear about certain principles of judgement of a horoscope. The signs, the houses and the planets in these are the three elements, as it were, which the astrologer takes up to interpret a chart but some other principles or rules of interpretation are also borne in mind by him. I will list the important ones below:

1. *Benefits and Malefics.* Though planets can become benefic or malefic by virtue of lordship, some have their own defined nature which is characteristic of them, wherever they are placed or whichever be the house owned by them. Thus, Sun, Mars, Saturn and Rahu are evil, Sun being the least and Rahu being the most. If they are located in the adverse or evil signs, they become even stronger to produce adverse results. If in their signs or in friendly signs or when they are exalted, they lose their evil nature.

The waxing Moon, Mercury, Venus and Jupiter are increasingly powerful benefics. Ketu is generally evil by nature.

The difference between Saturn and Mars is that while Saturn will cause a string of misfortunes, delays and disappointments in life, it will ultimately purify one's mind and lead to a deep understanding of human nature and take one away from the bonds of life and materialistic tendencies. Saturn will ultimately bring peace but not until you have stopped clinging to the materialistic life.

Mars on the other hand will constantly arouse passion and strife, reverses and losses, hurts and injury, to the end of one's life, peace being as far away at the end as it was in the beginning.

2. All planets in the 8th and 12th will produce evil results.

3. Evil planets when located in the 3rd, 6th or 11th house produce beneficial results.

4. Retrograde planets become more powerful than they are when in direct forward motion.

5. Planets located in trines become more powerful and if lords of angles are located in trines, they become very powerful for producing good results. A planet that is lord of an angle as well as a trine is the most powerful of all.

6. Lord of the ascendant will always produce good results.

7. If the lord of trines and angles and more particularly 9th and 10th and the 4th and 5th exchange position—that is if the 10th lord is in the 9th and the 9th lord in the 10th or the 4th in the 5th and the 5th in the 4th—such a configuration will produce a powerful beneficial yoga which will lift the native to a high position in their mutual periods and sub-periods. This holds good even if one of the planets is evil or adverse by nature or lordship or sign position.

8. Rahu and Ketu give results according to the lord of the sign in which they are located. Their results are also modified by the planet aspecting them. Thus, Rahu and Ketu if located in Aries will give results which Mars the sign lord is to give. If in Leo, the result will be of Sun, the sign lord. Also if they are conjoined with a planet, the power of the planet to give good or bad results will be absorbed by Rahu or Ketu which in their periods and sub-periods will produce the results of the planet. It

is as if that planet had surrendered all its powers to Rahu and Ketu.

9. Planets close to the Sun become combust and lose their power to produce results.

10. The Sun rules the soul, wordly position, health and father. Moon rules the mother and the mind. Mars rules brothers, courage, enemy and the earth (that is landed property). Mercury has sway over the intellect and the ability for speedy execution of work. Jupiter rules over son, physique and wealth. Venus rules the wife, jewellery, vehicle and love. Saturn has connection with hindrances, misfortune, old age and service. Evil planets such as lords of the 8th and the 12th lose their power to produce evil results if they are debilitated.

11. Saturn's aspect reduces and may even nullify the results which the aspected planet would otherwise produce.

12. Mars and Saturn are bitter enemies but in the planetary war between them, Saturn vanquishes Mars. Saturn, by its 3rd or 7th or 10th aspect on Mars will nullify the latter's power to produce any result, good or bad. However, if Mars aspects Saturn by its 4th or 8th aspect, Saturn does not lose its powers —good or bad.

13. Planets form two, mutually hostile, groups. One group consists of Sun, Jupiter, Mars and Moon and the other of Saturn, Mercury and Venus.

14. Jupiter is said to be the preceptor and guide of the gods. Venus is the preceptor and the guide of the *Asuras* or Demons. While the first has godly qualities the other rules over wordly goods and the material side of life.

15. The planets become strong or active at certain ages of a person's life. Thus, the Sun becomes active in the 22nd year,

Moon in the 24th, Mars in the 28th, Mercury in the 32nd, Jupiter in the 16th, Venus in the 25th, Saturn in the 36th and Rahu and Ketu in the 42nd year. Planets will start yielding the results they have to give at the above ages.

16. If in a chart, the 9th lord is located in the fifth house, this shows that the child has been conceived outside the marriage bond.

17. Saturn and Mars are both independent planets, setting their own norms and standards. They do not follow the man made laws or commandments. While Saturn goes about things quietly and secretly, Mars goes for open defiance, aggressive in its ways. This is why they become so important when connected with fifth house matters and with Venus.

If Uranus also has connection with the 5th house or with Venus, this will also lead to departure from the norms laid down by society as Uranus stands for unconventionality and originality. It does not care for the rules of society.

18. If in any horoscope the planets are scattered as if in a thin string with no house containing more than one planet, this makes a weak horoscope and one has difficulty in rising from a more or less lowly position in life. As no house has more than one planet there is no focussing of the planetary forces in any house and one is a helper or messenger or lift man or a servant or an unskilled worker in some organisation. Even if he has some talent, he will not be able to take any advantage of it, for opportunities will not come his way and he will remain condemned to a comparatively lowly station in life.

19. If in a horoscope the lords of the 6th, 8th and 12th are located in one or more of these three houses, this is a factor for good fortune and rise in life even though the rest of the chart does not indicate rise in life.

The Planets

At the time of the evolution of Hindu astrology, the newer planets Uranus, Neptune and Pluto were unknown and were therefore not taken into account but Rahu and Ketu (Dragon's head and Dragon's tail) were known and that they were not real bodies was also known. The Sun and the Moon, though not planets in the sense that the others are, in Hindu astrology are dealt with as if they too are planets.

The Sun

The Sun of course is central in the planetary system and together with the planets forms a vast system. The influence of the Sun can be felt by our physical senses—the heat and light coming from it being felt by us all. The colours are also present in sunlight and so also a great variety of other rays not obvious to our senses—such as the ultraviolet radiations and the long waves beyond those causing heat. Magnetic and ionic influences of the Sun are also not known to us at all.

Since the Sun is the primal creator of our solar system, it is appropriately considered to be the soul of Kalpurusha, its essential and basic nature.

The Sun stands for one's eyesight and the heart. It gives mastery, nobility of character, command, cheerfulness, trustfulness and as it represents the King, it is indicative of government service. Sun in the 10th house is a strong indication of service in some government department. In the

11th, Sun gives friends and acquaintances in high places. In the 12th the Sun causes one to live in places away from the place of birth. It also gives near total change of surroundings. In the second it may give good income from public or government funds and allied sources. In the third it gives great courage and the ability to withstand the "slings and arrows of outrageous fortune" as Shakespeare has put it. In the sixth, it weakens the constitution but destroys one's enemies. In the 8th it gives public death in the sense that death is reported in the media.

The Moon

It is the mind of Kalpurusha. It stands for the mother and for women in general.

The Moon is exalted in Taurus in which one of its Nakshatras—Rohini—is located. It is said that Moon is happiest when in this nakshatra. As the Moon is highly receptive, one's qualities will undergo changes according to the planet conjoined with the Moon. Thus, Mars gives excessive activity, aggression and some proneness to accidents. With Venus it gives love of the arts, fine clothing and accentuates the emotional side. With Saturn it gives caution, pessimism, depression and worry. With the Buddhist monk, one will keep chanting "all is sorrow, all is misery."

One's mental powers are strangely and adversely affected if Moon is close to Ketu, that is within two or three degrees of it. The mind becomes abnormal and even insane. This is a highly undesirable combination as it leads to some sort of abnormality when the periods of Moon and Ketu operate, even if a person at birth or early childhood appears to be normal.

By house position the Moon when nearly full gives a pleasing appearance when it is in the ascendant. In the second it gives variable income. In the third one may have sisters. In the fifth it produces an emotional nature. In the seventh it gives a beautiful wife or a good looking husband. In the 10th one may change his profession many times. In the 11th one may have many female acquaintances. In the 12th the Moon gives some seclusion or life in a secluded place away from the hubbub of cities.

The central importance attached to the Moon in Hindu astrology is clear from the fact that the Moon's position in the 27 nakshaktras is determined by all astrologers to ascertain the ruling planet or the dasha lord at the time of birth. The balance of the dasha or the number of years the period of the dasha lord has yet to run is entered in the natal chart and then the periods of the subsequent dasha lords, in serial order, for the entire estimated life span. The full periods are :-

Ketu	7	years
Venus	20	years
Sun	6	years
Moon	10	years
Mars	7	years
Rahu	18	years
Jupiter	16	years
Saturn	19	years
Mercury	17	years

The total comes to 120 years. In the most unlikely event of one surviving this span of 120 years, the dashas will be repeated. These dashas are also named after Parashar the sage who is believed to have first enumerated them.

Mercury

Mercury is the planet nearest to the Sun and moves around the Sun in an elliptical orbit, turning the same face to the Sun at all times as the moon does to the earth. As it is very near to the Sun, it is visible only for a short time just before sunrise in the east and just after sunset in the west.

The ancient Greeks were aware of the duality of Mercury that one half of it shines in the sunlight and the other half is in perpetual shadow. They visualised it as a youth dressed half in black and half in white, with wings in his feet. He was called the messenger of the gods.

Mercury is able to take on the nature of the planet with which it is conjoined and becomes more benefic if that planet is a benefic and it becomes adverse if that planet is evil.

Mercury governs one's intellect and has a quick grasp and equally quick wit. If in the ascendant it gives a sense of humour, verbal ability, talkativeness and the ability to see to the bottom of things in a quick flash. It loves variety to the extent of being inconstant in human relations. It owns the signs Gemini and Virgo but appears to be more in accord with Gemini than with Virgo in its essential nature. Adversely affected Mercurians will be liars and gamblers and can easily take to the poisoned pen, writing anonymous letters. Their perpetual chatter bores others.

Mercury rules the direction North and in Numerology its number is 5. Mercurians apppear to be younger than they are and even in an advanced age retain much of their youthful agility.

Apart from such professions as journalism and publicity, Mercurians also make good accountants, telephone and telegraph personnel, stenographers and personal assistants, salesmen and when Virgo is also connected, they go for petty trades, shop owners and partnerships.

Mercury's colour is green.

Venus

It is the most brilliant object in the night and is also visible as the morning or the evening star upto 3 hours before sunrise or after sunset.

Venus is a feminine planet ruling the softer side of man. It rules Taurus and Libra and is exalted in Pisces. If it is in the ascendant, it will bestow soft looks, pleasing manners and a peaceful nature. It gives harmony, attractiveness and a diplomatic nature with the ability to restore peace in a warlike or a quarelling group.

Venus is the supreme lord of love and affection and Venus controlled persons will begin their love life early. Women in particular with strong and well placed Venus will be romantically inclined and will seek emotional bonds from an early age, with more than one partner. Their need for love is deeply ingrained and they will all the time appear to be seeking it wherever they can find it not because of any perversity but because love and romance mean everything important in life to them. Life will appear to be empty and meaningless to them unless their deep hunger for emotional love is satisfied.

Venus adversly placed and when connected with health and diseases will lead to diseases of the reproductive system, venereal and skin which spoil one's appearence.

Venus has much to do with gems and jewellery, fine clothes, the fashion industry, drama and cinema, modelling and also with fine arts.

In the second house Venus will yield wealth with little effort. In its dasha it will give all kinds of luxuries and comfort. In the third, it may give musical ability, singing and female siblings. In the fourth, Venus will give vehicles, properties and a peaceful home. In the fifth Venus is indicative of artistic ability, creativeness and if associated with Saturn and Mars and also if with Uranus, a generalised and constant hunger for the opposite sex, some examples of which are given elsewhere in this book.

In the sixth Venus may give good service indicated by sign position and aspects. In the seventh Venus is generally an important factor for a good spouse, good looking and knowing the art of satisfying the partner. In the eighth Venus will lead to insults due to the opposite sex and also makes one generous even to the extent of taking off one's coat and giving it to the poor supplicant. In the ninth Venus will be generally indicative of good fortune. In the tenth Venus shows a career in the arts, films, theatre, fashion etc. In the eleventh it gives gains, friends amongst women and makes one potent and usually a person with several children. In the case of women with 11th house Venus, fertility will be good and they wll conceive quickly. The twelfth house Venus is said to increase the pleasure of the bed and the bedroom.

Mars

It is the planet of energy and courage. It gives warlike qualities, aggressive energy, combativeness as well as good looks, youthfulness, passion and an independent spirit, fond of leadership. Mars is reddish in appearance in the night sky and gives one a ruddy complexion when in the ascendant.

Mars gets exalted in Capricorn and debilitated in Moon's sign Cancer. When adversely aspected it makes one quarrelsome, violent and very aggressive. It also produces many violent criminals, drunkards and sexual perverts, to the extent of enjoying the giving of pain to others, like Marquis de Sade. They make dangerous enemies and it is not wise to rub them the wrong way as they have the knack of coming out victorious in every warlike situation.

The ancient Romans worshipped Mars as the God of War. This is not surprising, for the great Romans of history were all talented generals such as Julius Ceaser and Antony. Of Julius Ceaser it is said that though he fought in many wars, he never suffered even a scratch until the day of his death when his son attacked him with a dagger. Ceaser was so aghast that he is said to have given up resistance saying "Et tu, Brute !!."

Alexander the Great was another great general and conqueror whom Mars had taken under his wings.

Mars rules landed property. He is also said to be a thief. If Mars is in the 12th house, one will lose things by thefts and will himself be inclined to be thievish and even a shoplifter. In the ascendant, Mars gives much energy and daring but may also cause injuries and cuts. In the second house one will be reckless in spending money. In the third it gives great courage and the power of resistance but is adverse for younger brothers. If adverse in the fourth house, it denotes loss of property. In the fifth house, it causes quarrel with the son while its influence on one's sexual life is for excess and loss of control on one's senses. In the sixth, Mars is adverse for one's enemies but may also result in fevers and all acute conditions of bad health. In the seventh Mars generates quarrels with people one comes in contact with and is also adverse for marital accord. In the eighth, loss of spouse is indicated in the period or sub-period of Mars, if there is no beneficial influence operating on this house. In the ninth,

Mars may cause adverse conditions for the father, misadventures abroad or in long journeys. In the tenth Mars is said to be very good for one's career in a line associated with Mars, such as the armed forces, mechanical engineering, slaughter houses, etc.

Mars is of special importance in the life of women as they deal with fire (in the kitchen), bleeding and with temper in men. They have to learn much caution and tact and it is advisable for them to pray inwardly to Mars as frequently as possible to protect them and their loved ones from all types of injury, losses and harm and also from aggressive behaviour, assault and molestation on the part of the other men.

Jupiter

The largest planet in the solar system is given beneficial properties both in the western and Hindu system. In the west, Jupiter is considered to be the greater fortune, Venus being the lesser. This is true in the sense that while Venus can give such pleasures as fine clothes, jewellery, furniture, good food and the pleasures of the bed, Jupiter bestows righteousness, religious tendencies, qualities of a good teacher and healer, nobility of character and benevolence towards humanity. It saves and protects the native from physical harm and gives providential escape from situations of near disaster.

Jupiter is a giant among the planets. It is thus in the fitness of things that it should give excessive energy, rapid and excessive growth even to the extent of producing tumours.

Jupiterians are jovial and optimistic by nature. They love sports and are themselves good in sports. They can initiate and run large projects whether in government or private companies. They make good judges and the profession of medicine and teaching holds special attraction for them.

Jupiter in the ascendant will give an excess of energy or of physical growth. If the former they will be tireless, a human dynamo. In later life they may put on much fat specially if Jupiter is in the 10th house.

Jupiter is exalted in Cancer. It rules Sagittarius and Pisces. If located in the 9th, Jupiter will give providential help at all times and also make one deeply religious, in a higher sense, without any sectarian and denominational approach. In the second it will give much income by rightful means. In the 11th it gives contacts and friendship with persons high up in society such as ministers, senators, judges and so on. Its location in any of the angular houses 1st, 4th, 7th and 10th is said to be so beneficial that no evil planet can cause them any harm. In the trines (5th and 9th) Jupiter aspects the ascendant by its special aspects) (9th and 5th) and this too gives life-long beneficial affects.

Its divine nature can also be inferred from its names—Jove and Zeus. The last name has close affinity with Theos and Devas of Sanskrit which means god.

Saturn

It is the outermost planet visible to the naked eye. It is exalted in Libra and debilitated in Aries. This is just the opposite of Sun's exaltation and debilitation, for the Sun is exalted in Aries and debilitated in Libra. This also justifies the belief that though Saturn is the son of Sun, both are bitter enemies. This enmity is further proved by the mutually opposing qualities of the two for the Sun is hot while Saturn is very slow in its effects which however are long lasting. Saturn is a secretive planet, causing delays and disappointments. When Saturn is a benefic it gives much only after patient and continued labour. One has to approach Saturn with respect and not in a light hearted or frivolous manner and one must also remember that Saturn gives only when the aspirant is deserving for Saturn is a just planet.

Saturn also rules old age and asceticism. If it aspects Mars and Moon the wordly nature of Mars is suppressed and the mind controlled by Moon turns away from wordly pleasures. One becomes a strict task master, frugal in habits and food and disciplined. Life is organised by a fixed routine as in the case of the great philosopher Emmanuel Kant of whom it is said that people would set their watches when he came out for a stroll after his breakfast. Such people dislike pomp, speak to the point and even when they are very rich, they do without any kind of luxury.

Saturn rules the colour blue and the number 8. It is lame and slightly deaf. It causes diseases which develop slowly and take a long time to cure. It is bony and long limbed. It also governs products of mines, leather and wood.

Saturn in the ascendant slows down all processes, except when it is exalted. In the second it limits one's wealth and income and in the third, one's siblings. As Saturn also governs lands, together with Mars, when in the fourth house it gives one landed property though late in life. Its fifth house effects have been dealt with elsewhere in this book. In the sixth it produces lingering and chronic diseases which take a long time to cure. In the seventh Saturn causes adverse relations with the spouse and delays in marriage. In the eighth house while Saturn gives long life, it delays the process of death. One may go into a coma or be paralysed for many months or even years before death comes to the rescue. In the ninth Saturn gives a deeply philosophical attitude and also produces archaeologists. In the tenth Saturn makes one struggle for success and progress in life which comes slowly and after much effort and disappointment. In the eleventh it limits gains and one has few friends who are always not reliable. One has to achieve things by his own effort, without much help coming one's way. Saturn in the eleventh is also indicative of extra-marital relations as Saturn does not follow any man-made laws or rules of behaviour. In the 12th Saturn is generally wholly evil in the results it gives. It makes one arrogant and opinionated and one is usually the cause of his own fall because of fool-hardy behaviour.

In general appearance Saturn resembles the traditional picture of Uncle Sam, tall, thin and bony.

Uranus

It was unknown to the ancients. It was discovered in the 18th century and it takes 84 years to go round the Sun, remaining in one sign for 7 years. It is the planet of originality, unconventionality, sudden developments and also accidents, electricity and electric shocks, aviation and inventiveness. Uranus persons fall in love quickly and go for divorce equally quickly. The effects by house position can be made out if one remembers its basic nature. In the ascendant it gives independent thinking, eccentricity and inventiveness. In the second there are many ups and downs in income. In the third accidents may occur while on a journey. In the fourth trouble or dispute about property matters. In the fifth it gives secret love affairs, unconventional sex and in women dangerous birth or death of a child and in sixth it gives little understood diseases of an acute nature and in women it may give hysterical tendencies if Uranus is in an airy or a fiery sign. In the seventh "Marry in haste and repent at leisure." In the eighth the end comes quickly and one has to guard against accidents. In the ninth mental exploration in the realm of philosophy and spirituality. In the tenth Uranus gives inventive genius and creates a mind which sees reality in a way different from the usual. One does not go in a rut nor does one follow the beaten path. In the eleventh Uranus is all for strange friendship with either sex. In the twelfth house Uranus inclines one to psychic experience, secret enmity and losses which come about all of a sudden.

Neptune

It has been known for about 150 years. It completes one revolution around the Sun in about 146 years, staying in a sign for about 14 years.

As compared to the earth, Neptune too is a giant planet with a diameter of over 27,000 miles as against 8,000 miles of the earth and only 3,200 miles of Mercury. While the average distance of Mercury from the Sun is 36 million miles and of the earth 93 million miles, Neptune is about 2,800 million miles away, that is, 30 times as far away when compared to the distance of the earth. Now to us on earth the Sun appears to be the size of a football. On Neptune and more so on Pluto, it will be of the size of a large orange or a cricket ball. If we could stand on Neptune and Pluto, it would be hard to believe that an object of the size of a cricket ball in the heavens could exert such powerful force on these planets so as to keep them bound in its gravitational field and exert on them other powerful electromagnetic forces. And if we concede that this is indeed the case, we should have no difficulty in conceding also that Venus, for example, which is so much nearer to the earth does exert a powerful influence on us. So also the other planets such as Mars, Jupiter and Saturn. One should take a purely commonsense view of this matter without getting involved in dogmatic arguments. And the common sense view is that if a small object (as the Sun appears from Neptune and Pluto) 3,000 million miles away can influence them surely,

Venus only 25 million miles away could influence us too on earth (from earth to Venus the distance is about 25 million miles). This digression was necessary to point out that gravity and many of the other forces in the Universe have not been fully understood. Until they are, we should have an open mind.

Neptune governs all matters connected with the oceans as it is the lord of the sea. It has much to do with psychic forces, mediumship and unusual powers. The lower type of persons with Neptune influences may be licentious, treacherous and drug addicts. Its influence in the various signs and houses are not yet fully understood though it gives an element of mystery and unreliability wherever it is found.

Pluto

The god of the underworld and of death is as yet something of a mystery and little is known about its effects in signs and houses. In general it can be said that it emphasises matters concerning the house in which it is located. Some ascribe to it far reaching changes, regeneration and even death.

Rahu and Ketu

Apart from the planets proper, these two nodes of the Moon also play an important part in one's nativity. Both are generally considered to be evil in nature and produce adverse effects. An important characteristic of these nodes is that they, sort of, absorb the powers, for good or evil, of the planets with whom they are associated by conjunction or aspect. Thus, if with Mars they will in their periods or sub-periods, produce the effects which otherwise Mars would have caused and Mars' own periods and sub-periods will be to a large extent rendered ineffective.

Ketu is said to be like Mars in the effects it produces and is causative of hurts and injuries, wounds and cuts and even operations in its period or sub-periods. In the ascendant it gives belief in superstitions, in prayer and in magical practices such as those followed in many Arican societies. In the seventh Ketu produces abnormalities in the generative system often leading to surgery. It is adverse for married life in this house. Rahu in the 7th is also an unfavourable influence for married life and the spouse.

Though evil by nature, Rahu and Ketu will be influences for good if they are conjoined with benefics or with lord of benefic houses such as the 9th and 10th. Their Nakshatra position is also of great importance when one is studying the influence in the natal chart.

Rahu is said to rule over serpents and also over creepy, crawly creatures, insects, bugs, ants and over Muslims and Buddhists. If Rahu is in Scorpio then in its period and sub-period one is certain to come across such pests, one will make friends with Muslims or have a Muslim tenant or visit Islamic countries. Rahu also has domain over snake-charmers and donkeys. Under its influence one can become a sodomite and even have intercourse with quadrupeds.

Ketu's adverse influence on the mind when it is close to the moon has already been referred to. This produces symptoms of lunacy and in backward areas of the world, one still goes to the exorcist and to the witch doctor for help in treating the victim of such conditious instead of resorting to proper medical treatment. There is something in the behaviour of such patients which leads one to believe that they have been possessed by an evil spirit. Ketu is, therefore, said to control evil spirits, ghosts, hobgoblins and what not and arouses fear in the mind.

Fortuna

This too is not a planet but a point in the ecliptic that is found to be of importance for matters connected with worldly gains and material benefits. No chart should be taken as complete until Fortuna or the Part of Fortuna has been calculated and entered in it.

The part of Fortuna the symbol of which is the same as the symbol for the Earth (⊗) is calculated by adding the rising degree of the Ascendant taken from 0 degree Aries to the longitude of Moon also taken from the First point of Aries and then deducting the longitude of the Sun, again taken from 0^0 Aries. It will be seen that Fortuna is in the ascendant on new moon and in the seventh at full Moon. In whichever house it is found, it indicates good fortune through the matters indicated by that house. Thus, if in the Ascendant one gains by his or her own efforts. In the third one gains through brothers, neighbours, short journeys and so on. In the fourth one gains through landed property, in the 5th through young people, children and speculation, in the 7th through partners or the opposite sex, in the 11th through brothers and friends and so on.

THE NAKSHATRAS' INFLUENCE OVER PLANETS

The Nakshatras have been known in India for thousands of years and are referred to in the Vedas. During the days of the epic Mahabharata too they were widely known and it is believed that the epic war took place when the vernal equinox was in Krittika Nakshatra (as against the First degree of Aries as in the present times) about 27^0 away from the First point of Aries. As the rate of precession of the equinoxes is 72 years per degree, the age of the Mahabharata is at least 27×72 or about 1,900 to 2,000 years ago. As all Nakshatras are 13^0 20" in extension, this age could be another 72×13 or 936 years earlier or about 1000^0 B.C.

Nakshatras are the Lunar mansions, the moon moving from one to the next Nakshatra in about 24 hours completing the journey through the 27 Nakshatras in 27 days. As we learnt earlier, every Nakshatra has been assigned to one of the planets, Aswini to Ketu, Bharani to Venus, Krittika to the Sun and so on till we come to Aslesha the 9th Nakshatra which is ruled by Mercury. This completes four signs or 120^0 from 0^0 Aries and also the first 9 Nakshatras each Nakshatra being of 13^0 20" extension in the Zodiacal belt. Thereafter the next cycle of nine Nakshatras starts, beginning again with Ketu's Nakshatra, Magha in the sign Leo and followed by Purvaphalguni ruled by Venus, Uttaraphalguni ruled by Sun and so on till we come to Jyeshtha ruled by Mercury in Scorpio sign ruled by Mars and completing the second cycle of four signs or 120^0 ending at 240^0 Thereafter the third or last cycle starts with Moola Nakshatra again ruled by Ketu, followed by Purvashada ruled by Venus and so on to Revati the last of the 27 Nakshatras, ruled by Mercury and extending from 16^0 40" of Pisces to 30^0 of Pisces.

Now in this distinctly Indian system of astrology it is held that any planet in a particular Nakshatra is under the influence of the lord of the Nakshatra. Thus, the planet in Bharani will be under the influence of Venus and will produce results predominantly of Venus as it becomes an agent of Venus. A planet in Purvashada which is again a Nakshatra ruled by Venus but in Sagittarius ruled by Jupiter will also be under the sway of Venus.

Thus, the astrologer has to take the influence of the Nakshatra lord also into account when delineating horoscope influences—otherwise his analysis will be incomplete and in many cases quite wrong if he goes entirely and exclusively by the sign position of planets.

Western astrology is not aquainted with this Nakshatra system. In practice it is found that it gives remarkably accurate readings of the natal chart. We must, therefore, in all cases give in the natal chart the Nakshatra position of all the planets and one who studies such charts must see how the house or sign positions of planets are modified by the Nakshatra position.

CASTING THE HOROSCOPE

The following data are required for erecting an astrological or natal chart:

(a) The place of birth (for the long. and lat.)

(b) The date of birth

(c) The time of birth

In addition the ephemeris for the year of birth should also be available as also the Table of Houses or at least the Table of Ascendants.

The place of birth is important as it affects the time as well as the ascending sign (the Ascendant) and also the meridian or the 10th house.

The date of birth is essential for reading the planetary positions from the ephemeris for that particular day.

The time is essential for determining the degree rising in the eastern horizon at the moment of birth.

The place of birth may be east or west of the place for which the standard time has been laid down. Also it may be east or west of Greenwich for which G.M.T is readily available. Thus a person born in India might be born at a place east of 82^0 30' longitude or west of it. Indian Standard Time is valid and correct for the longitude 82^0 30' and is 5 hours 30 minutes ahead of G.M.T. If a person is born, say, at noon at longitude 82^0 30' the time in Indian Standard Time (I.S.T.) will also be the local mean time. If born at Delhi, when it is noon at 82^0 30' it will be only 11:40 a.m. Local Mean Time (L.M.T.) because the longitude of Delhi is 77^0 12', that is 5^0 18' less than the place for which I.S.T is fixed. Thus, one has to add or subtract 4 minutes for every degree that is more or less than 82 degrees 30' as the place of birth is east or west of 82^0 30'. At Dum Dum near Calcutta the L.M.T. is about 24 minutes more than I.S.T. as it is about 6 degrees east Of 82^0 30'. In Hyderabad in Andhra Pradesh the time will be 16 minutes less than I.S.T. as it is 4 degrees west of 82^0 30'.

Central European Time is 1 hour ahead of G.M.T. In the east coast of U.S.A the time interval is 5 hours (less than G.M.T). In Alaska, the interval is 8 hours.

The first step thus is to determine the Local Mean Time which will enable you to find out the exact ascendant.

The date of birth is obviously important as the Sun as well as the other planets keep changing their positions day to day (the Sun about 1^0 per day and the Moon upto about 15 degrees per day). From the ephemeris (in India many Panchangs are available giving the ascendants as well as the positions of Planets for every day of the year) note the planetary positions. From the Table of Houses or the Table of ascendants given in Panchangs, note down the rising degree and sign for the required date.

Thus, the ascendant and the sign position of all the planets will be known and all you have to do is to draw the chart and enter in it the ascendant and the planets.

Next you should also note down the Nakshatra positions of all the planets starting with the Moon which will give you the balance of the period or the dasha operating at birth. Subsequent Dashas should also be noted, giving also the dates from which they will be operative. If you wish to go into further detail, you could also work out the aspects. Some ephemerises also give the aspects to the moon as well as the aspects between the planets, for every day of the year and if such an ephemeris is available to you, your labour will be saved to a great extent.

You will notice that the position of the Sun in the natal chart gives you the approximate time of birth. Thus, if Sun is located in the ascendant one is born around sunrise; if the Sun is in the fourth house, birth is around midnight. If in the seventh, birth is around sunset and in the tenth around midday. Mercury will always be close to the Sun, at the most in the preceding or the succeeding sign. Venus which is never more than 48^0 from the Sun will never be more than two signs away. Thus, if one is born with Sun in Gemini, Venus will be in Aries or Taurus or Gemini or Cancer or Leo but never in Libra or Sagittarius. This provides a cross-check on the accuracy of the chart.

The chart once correctly made will be of permanent use when analysing or delineating one's character and personality, as described in the relevant chapters of this book. The time spent on casting it accurately will be well spent.

The sign position of the planets for the day of birth will be available from the ephemeris or Panchang and can be copied out without any difficulty. One should in addition draw up a chart for the house positions also, as the house position may or may not be the same as the sign position. In a recent case, for instance, I found in a chart that while by signs, Saturn was in the 11th (i.e., 11th sign from the ascending sign) by house position it was in the 10th. If for instance the 24th degree of a sign is rising and Saturn is in the 8th degree, while it may be in the 11th sign, by house position it will be in the 10th. The results of Saturn in the 10th will be quite different from those indicated by Saturn in the 11th. In most cases it will be found that Saturn will give both the results—that is of the 11th as well as of the 10th.

So also with other planets. In giving a reading, the astrologer must refer to both the charts—that is the one by sign position and the chart by the house position. Much experience is necessary in such cases for a correct evaluation of the chart.

It may be added here that the various ephemerises and the Panchangs published in India give the planetary positions for the time mentioned clearly in the ephemerises or Panchang, usually 5:30 a.m. for the latter, i.e., midnight GMT. Some ephemerises will give the position for 12 noon GMT. As birth can occur at any time of the day, some calculation becomes necessary to find the exact position of the planet. If birth is at 11 a.m. and the Panchang has given the positions of planets at 5:30 a.m., the motion of the planets for 5½ hours has to be worked out and added to the position given in the panchang. Some ephemerises give the daily motion of the Moon and other planets. If this is not given, you will have to calculate it, taking the two 24-hour readings from the given tables which will give the daily motion. From this you have to calculate the motion for the number of hours till the hour of birth.

You will notice that the motion of planets varies from day to day. Sometime the planet is stationary. It can also get retrograde, in which case the degrees and minutes you calculate will have to be deducted from the figures given in the ephemeris or Panchang. If a planet is retrograde, this should be noted in the chart you prepare as retrograde planets are said to be weak.

You must note also that Rahu and Ketu are always retrograde in their motion. The Sun and Moon are never retrograde.

Sex And Astrology

It can truly be said that this is an age of sex. Sex dominates our culture—our literature, our clothes, our songs, our media. Not that in earlier times sex did not exist or was of little consequence. It was after all sex that was at the basis of most wars and 'the face that launched a thousand ships' was the centre of attraction in those times. The great Greek conquerer Alexander was a man known for his orgies in one of which, when drunk, he killed his best friend and general. Mark Antony too was a great general in his times known for the orgies he organised with the ladies of Cleopatra's court, though Cleopatra herself never, as her biographer has pointed out, went for the men or allowed them to possess her. She was a great queen and was conscious of this and never lost her balance or her dignity among the sordid and lascivious goings on at these orgies.

Another great conqueror was William the Norman, said to have possessed an extraordinarily large organ which is shown in its active form in the famous Norman Tapestries.

In modern times several important persons have been known for their sexual activities. President Kennedy is said to have been active sexually with a number of women even though he was married to a beautiful and talented woman. Another President is said to have organised parties at his ranch where the various rooms occupied by women he invited for the parties could not be bolted or locked from the inside and he visited more than one during a night. Even Clinton has been charged with using his position as Governor of Arkansas for getting young women to bed.

It is not only men who have been known for over-active sex. Women too are known for such behaviour. A great Russian Empress is said to have kept men exclusively for her sexual satisfaction, beheading them when she got tired of them in the manner of Haroon Al Rashid who wanted a different woman every night and could not tolerate the idea of any one else sharing her favours, so that he had no choice but to have them killed the next morning. Clive, the man who laid the foundations of the British Empire in India is said to have wanted 'a lakh and a lass' every day combining his greed with his lust.

What is it in the astrological charts of such persons which can reveal their true nature in spite of the outwardly composed, polite and even polished exterior? The astrologer is under some limitation in understanding such persons and even when he gets a clue to their sexual nature he cannot verify his reading or assessment of such persons for we are normally reticent in matters of sex. The best situation for the astrologer will be one in which he could ask the subject or visitor to strip so that the degree of correlation between the planetary positions and the physical nature of the visible sex organs could be studied. But in the case of his women subjects, even if they stripped for his examination, he would not be able to form any useful opinion since the sexually active parts of a woman are all hidden from view.

We have all heard of the proverbial Arab Sheikh whose insatiable sexual appetite drove him to keep a large number of women in his harem. What about women? Nature has not made man and woman in such a different way that one is promiscuous and frequently over-sexed while the other is monogamous and sexually more or less frigid. Differences in this matter are mainly due to the cultural milieu in which women grow up. A friend of mine for instance was so made that he was driven to possess or try to possess every female he came across, young or old. He was married when he was nineteen, to a girl who was barely thirteen. The very first night he went for her, with such energy and violence that her vargina got ruptured and had to be stitched up at the hospital the next morning. He kept up such behaviour throughout his life and died before he was 55. His wife came to hate sex. She longed for romantic love of which my friend was not capable for he always rushed into the act without any preliminaries and without any foreplay to arouse his wife. She confided to me that he sometimes went for sex upto 17 times in a day.

A woman I came across once was also similarly made and she could have an orgasm over 36 times during the course of a single session, with a man who could not hold himself further and gave in, in a final moment of ecstasy. She was however, still not exhausted and could have gone on for several more orgasms. This example shows that over-sexed women are even more active than over-sexed men and can leave the proverbial Arab Sheikh far behind in the matter of their capacities. Woman in this respect is certainly not the weaker sex. This is a matter which I leave to my female readers who will be in a better position to form a correct opinion.

When the astrologer tries to study such subjects, he finds that the dominating planets are Venus, Mars, Saturn and Uranus, the dominating houses being 5,11, and 7. During my 30 years experience I have found that if for instance, Venus, Mars and Saturn are combined in the 5th house by actual conjunction or by aspect and if Jupiter is not intervening to save the situation, the subject will be loose in his morals, as they say. He or she will be promiscuous, ever ready to have sex with all and sundry. A woman subject with such a combination will be one who says "No one can ravish me for I am so willing,' a pushover.

Mae West is said to have got up from her husband's bed the very first night as she had an uncontrollable appetite for sex. She got up and looked for other men, whether a lift-man or a cab-driver or a hotel boy mattered little. All she was looking for was a man who could have sex with her.

Another woman I came across some years ago had this configuration of Mars, Saturn and Venus in the 5th house, but aspected by Jupiter. She lost her virginity well before marriage but the man later married her. Still, Jupiter's influence could save the situation only in part and she became the mistress of a very rich businessman with the knowledge and consent of her husband. This rich man has helped the couple all along and has also financed her children's studies. He still takes her along in his business trips, sometimes also with her husband.

Those who are doubters or those not acquainted with astrology and its principles should study the above fifth house combinations, for it can be said that the rule regarding the fifth house occupied by Mars, Venus and Saturn but not aspected by Jupiter, is as true as the Second Law of Thermodynamics or the Law of Gravity or any other law of the Physical Sciences. There is no exception and there is no person born with such a combination who can restrain himself from "going astray" sexually. There are persons who used to organise or participate orgiastic parties that were becoming fashionable in the sixtees before the fear of AIDS drove them away. As is known, in these parties, men and women stripped and indulged in indiscriminate sex, even with complete strangers.

I am aware that such parties are still organised on a small scale, complete with blue films.

The fifth house as we will learn later controls one's love life, creativity, recreation and also procreation (children). Mars is a planet of great energy, it is active and dynamic, fearless and can even be violent. It does every thing openly. Saturn on the other hand is secretive, not trusting anyone. Saturn is also associated with Satan and like Satan is said to be like a satyr with an ever-erect organ. When these two are combined with Venus who is also Aphrodite or the goddess of Love, we get the situation mentioned above, particularly in the fifth house of love and procreation.

Apart from the 5th house, its opposite the 11th is also of importance for the 11th directly aspects the 5th by the powerful 7th house aspect. Planets in the 11th are also therefore taken into account in a study of the sexual nature of man. Western scholars are generally agreed that any of the major planets Mars, Saturn, Uranus and Neptune, if placed in the 11th, take one away from the straight and narrow path of monogamy, fidelity and so on. Venus in this house gives one great capacity for love and attracts women. Venus in the 5th house is also a centre of sexual attraction and a man with such a placement of Venus, particularly for Scorpio Ascendants when Venus becomes exalted in the 5th (being in Pisces) need make no effort to go woman hunting—they will come to him unsought and in droves as it were, one after the other. Such a person with exalted Venus in the 5th may be an artist, a painter, a poet or writer, an actor or a person active in any other creative line and naturally attracts women.

In the 7th house the situation is slightly different. The 7th is the house of the partner, the spouse or in short one's opposite number with whom one deals in any manner in life. It does not deal exclusively or even mainly with sexual matters or one's love life for which the 5th house has to be referred. In practice it is found that the 7th is adversely affected by any of the evil planets if located in it. Thus, Saturn will show some coldness between the partners, delay or hindrances in marriage, the age difference will be marked or the wife will be older than the husband. Mars in the 7th with its explosive energy will affect the relationship between the partners in a way that one may expect from Mars. In such couples there are frequent quarrels, the man uses force or the wife may want to be on top in the sexual act. They enjoy the act if there is some violence in it, an element of rape as it were. The man will use fist blows, his kisses will be more like bites and he will always use some kind of aggressive violence during the act. If Mars is also with another evil planet he will be a sadist. Readers may recall the case of the American young man charged with killing his girl friend. The man admitted that he enjoyed violence during the act and in the case of death of his friend he explained that on that occasion he used more than usual violence and the girl died as he gripped her throat during the act out there in the park to which they had gone for making love. He had no motive or desire for killing the girl—just that violence and sexual passion were so closely linked in his mental make-up that he normally came to hurt his sexual partner. The judge who tried the case let the man go with a warning. Obviously the judge was a man of deep understanding of human nature and also a judge of long experience.

Evil planets in the 7th can also affect the reproductive system. If Ketu or Dragons Tail be there with Saturn, the native can develop venereal diseases and may even lose his or her capacity to produce children. If with Rahu or Dragons Head there are quarrels and even long lasting antipathy. Rahu alone in the 7th, particularly in adverse signs such as Scorpio, will result in excessive indulgence in sex during youth but such a native in later life loses the capacity for sex and may become impotent.

Uranus the planet of originality and eccentricity will impel the native to unconventional sex. In the 5th house for instance Uranus will impel one not only to a certain degree of promiscuity but will also lead him to incestuous acts. If with Rahu he may even have sex with animals. In India, such a native will be attracted to the Tantric philosophy which holds that sex is the basic force in our lives and it is through sex that we can obtain liberation All our relationships with other human beings are temporary and may change in future births. Thus, brothers and sisters may have been husbands and wives in previous generations and may be fathers and daughters or mothers and sons in future births. Such relationships have no sanctity—all that is important and basic in our human situation is the fact of sexual attraction, for male and female are but two aspects of cosmic energy and uniting these two forces—the phallus and its female counterpart, *yoni* and *lingam, yang* and *yin, bolaka* and *kakkolaka* will lead to ultimate realisation of the supreme reality behind this entire visible world of which the senses are or can ever be aware. Let us not be trapped by the wrong and false concepts of wordly relationships—uncle and aunt, father and daughter, husband and wife, mother and son, brother and sister—but let us become aware of the duality in the world, a duality we have to overcome in our effort to reach supreme bliss which can come to us only by a direct and unitive experience or realisation of the ultimate Ground. It is this direct and unitive experience of the Divine Ground which will bring us self-realisation and will release us from the bondage of human existence. This is the philosophy that Uranus in the 5th will teach.

The Hindus have always held that there are several ways to reach God. This is what has made them so tolerant. The Muslim fundamentalist of the present times cannot tolerate or accept any view other than which he thinks is laid down in his religion. All other views and beliefs are to be destroyed totally —so the Holy war or Jehad, so the *fatwas* against Tasleema or Rushdie. But to the Hindu, let each one follow his own chosen path, let a hundred flowers bloom.

This disgression was necessary to explain how planetary positions not only affect our body and physical make-up but also modify our entire way of thinking. It can be said that Providence (or God if you like) has scattered all manner of things before us in this universe, an infinite variety of creatures, plants, stones and rocks, minerals, arts and crafts, beliefs and thoughts, creeds and disclipines. One person goes for biology, another for economics, a third for the army and so on. If I go for astrology is it not because in my horoscope Mercury or Jupiter are in the 9th house, if I am a writer, because Mercury and Gemini are important in my natal chart; if I am attracted towards poetry or the fine arts, is it not because Venus is in the 5th house?

How much free will do we have in such matters? Do we choose our beliefs or do these beliefs choose us because we are so made that they can fit into our astrological make up beautifully and can take us along the path of their own development.

I will leave the subject here, for the reader to ponder over the ideas I have referred to in this chapter and come to his own conclusion. I will only say that our entire mental and spiritual make up, the way we react to things, the ideas and beliefs we 'choose', in fact our entire *weltanschauung* is in a strange but definite way linked to the signs, planets and houses of our natal charts.

EPILOGUE

Astrology, as we have learnt, is built around the twelve signs, the twelve houses of the natal chart and the planets located in these signs and houses. It is only after a proper study of these three basic blocks with which astrology is built that one gathers some knowledge of the subject but it is experience that gives one some sort of mastery of the subject and the longer and more varied the experience, the better will be the understanding of the subject.

In studying the subject one has to leave behind him the tendency to place values on the signs, planets and houses. Though one talks of good and bad houses, benefics and malefics, one does not bring to bear on the persons whose natal charts one reads, any judgement of moral value. Certain results flow from a given configuration of planetary forces in the chart but these results are not to be judged in terms of human moral norms. Suppose a mosquito bites or stings a child who, after a few days develops high fever and who, if not treated in time, may die. In such a case we do not bring in judgement of values and say that the mosquito is an evil insect or that his act of stinging the child was an evil act. It is just that it is the mosquito's inherent nature to sting and suck blood on which its survival depends.

Astrological forces are blind like the laws of nature. They operate all the time. Some of the results they produce may be beneficial to us in which case we call them benefic influences or they may produce results that are adverse for us. In either case these forces are operative out there and are independent of our moral commandments or value judgments. The astrologer then should study these forces as they are in their essential nature and the more he does so the less will he be carried away by preconceived ideas of morality.

Astrology thus teaches us to take a broad and humane view of things. The vast panorama of life spreads out before him with its acts, feelings, motives and its pleasures and pains and the astrologer sees them dispassionately much as the Creator perhaps sees the world, with understanding, good will and compassion. He can offer counsel and in times of trouble, strife and mental suffering, he will be able to explain how most of the trouble is due to certain stellar influences and how these will cease when the period or the dasha of the afflicting planet comes to an end and the dasha of a favourable planet starts. He is thus in a position similar to that of the priest to whom one goes to confess his sins and who offers absolution in the name of God. The astrologer though not pretending to act in the name of God can offer much help to the poor sufferer and while explaining the nature of the influences that are causing suffering, arouse hope and courage in the person coming for consultation and enable him once more to stand up erect and face the strings and arrows of fortune with fortitude and with hope, for there is no cloud that does not have a silver lining. The astrologer will help one to see this lining and with hope once more in his breast say to himself, if winter has come, can spring be far behind?

It is my belief that one who has come thus far and has read this book with an open mind, will not be the same person that he was before he opened this book. If this is indeed the case, it will be a tribute not to me or to my powers of persuasion but to the truths of astrology.